CHANCE
OF A
LIFETIME

Jefffreyst1s

CHANTS OF A LIFETIME

SELECTED POETRY OF
LINCOLN BERGMAN
1953–2003

Front cover art from a painting by Miranda Bergman
Back cover author photograph by Joseph A. Blum
Graphic design on pages 17 and 174 by Deborah LeSueur
Famous 60s fist on page 295 by Frank Cieciorka from
The Movement newspaper.

Very special gratitude to dear friends Mark Merin and
Cathleen Williams for many things, including a very
generous contribution to help this book get printed.

Regent Press · Oakland, California

**This book is lovingly dedicated to
my two wonderful daughters
Anna Thai Binh and Caitlin Poema,
also to Mahealani,
and to all the children of the world.**

Even as I have known the selfless indefatigable love of a mother
Concerned only for the highest possible vitality of her children,
Leaving their lives free to them, not seeking to smother
Any jet of their spirits in her own preconceptions or wishes—
Would such were the love of every one of us for each other!

> Hugh MacDiarmid,
> Revolutionary Scottish poet

And for Edward Said and Rachel Corrie and their vision of justice.

©1995/2003 by LB Publications. All rights reserved.

Library of Congress Cataloging-in-Publication Data

Bergman, Lincoln.
    Chants of a lifetime : selected poetry of Lincoln
Bergman, 1953-2003.
       p. cm.
    ISBN 1-58790-057-2
     I. Title.

PS3552.E719344A6 2004
811'.54--dc22

2003066651

Manufactured in the U.S.A.
REGENT PRESS
6020–A Adeline Street
Oakland, CA 94608
regentpress@mindspring.com

Contents

Acknowledgments	9
A Few Words of Poetic Introduction	15
Start She Said / Opening Invocation	17
Just Pour It Out by Meridel Le Sueur	18
A Korean Baby by Anne Bergman	19
Frustration by Leibel Bergman	19
Invocation for a Green Thumb by Dorothy Broms	20
Great Profligate Poet	21
Rip Van Winkle	21
Introducing the Poet	22
My Lifelong Love Affair	23
Starting Out Again Tonight	24
Century Plant	25
The Frameups Shall Cease	27
Spectator	29
Fillmore Temple	29
Synagogue in Mourning	30
Cattle Ranch Operation	31
Deep Springs Revisited	32
For Walt Whitman	34
Mind on Freedom (for Tracy Sims)	35
Orange Apricot Brandy	37
An Old Riddle	37
Ithaca Graveyard	38
To Paul and Vietnam Protest at Cornell	41
Acropolitic Sunset (for Arlene)	43
The Night Was Long	45
To My Class in Peking	46
Four Limericks	47
The Curse	48
Dover Beach Revisited	49
Changsha (after Mao Tse-tung)	50
Letter to the Draft Board	51
Sky River	53
The Song of Hayakawa (or Up Against the Wall Mother Country)	55
Heavier Than Mount Tai (for Fred Hampton)	59
Another Day	64
Seeds of Revolution (for Jeff Sharlet)	65
To the Oakland 7 from the Oakland 10,000	68
In Memory of Al Lannon	71
In Contempt (for Bobby Seale)	72

A Way of Speaking	74
Song of a Thread (by Ho Chi Minh)	76
State of Emergency	77
Memorial to Nguyen Thai Binh	80
On to Victory (for Ho Chi Minh)	81
Sonnet for the Fall	83
The Perfume River (for My Loc)	84
They Are Bombing the Dikes	86
Prose Poem: Peace Agreement	88
Tet 1977: Rhetorical Question	89
Anti-War Rally: Golden Gate Park	89
This Country They Call Free	90
For Wounded Knee and Liberty	91
Attica (as broadcast)	92
Epitaph for J. Edgar Hoover	94
Never Let Them Force You to Forget	96
Drum Victory	96
Cuba Si	98
The Land Is Life	99
The Night Before Moncada	100
Guerrilla Couplets	104
Song of Puerto Rico	105
Confused and Mortal Beings (for Gayle)	106
In the Valley of Viñales	108
Red Curtains	109
Kinder Gentler Rock-A-Byes	109
Passover 1977	110
Anna's Birth Announcement	111
This Is A Proofreader	112
On Reading A Speech to a Meeting	113
Love Changes: Sonnet Amply Plagiarized	114
Optimistic Shakespeare	115
Sonnet on Writing	115
Sonnet on Friendship	116
Happy Birthday to Joe	117
Sonnet to Dorth and Will (40th Anniversary)	118
Birthday Sonnet to Dorothy	118
Sonnet for Wilbur Strong Broms	119
Sonnet for My Mother	120
To Hold Your Body	121
Auto-Immune Deficiency Blues	122
Written On the First Night of the Israeli Invasion of Lebanon	123
Blues for Beirut	127

Mantra Contra Contras	128
Haiku for John Santos	128
Contragate Rap	129
Sonnet for South Africa	132
Just After Ides of March 1985	133
Driving the Hearse	136
Naked at the Macintosh Computer	137
Sunday Morning	141
Labor Pains of A Witch	146
Ode to the Octopus	147
Black Orchid	148
Best Left Unsaid	148
A Labor of Love	149
A Strange Bloke	150
My Shortest Poem	150
Who Else But Bush	150
Pharoah Sanders at S.F. State	151
Of Human Imperfection (All I Ask)	154
Beginnings and Endings (for Efrem)	156
There is a Time	157
I Will Always Remember You Singing	
(for Dick Broadhead)	158
Land of Lakes	160
Collective Poem #1: Childhood Memories	162
For Elsa with Love	167
Love Sky for Lisa	170
Oyster Ecstasy	171
The Land of What If	172
Ecstasy	173
To Deborah and the Goddess of the Clay	175
Caitlin's Birth Announcement	177
Toucan Do	177
A Child's First Christmas in Berkeley	178
Selections from Redwood Rhapsodies	180
Rock of Wages	184
Yom Kippur 1988	185
Preparing for My Father's Death	186
Love Sonnet to My Father After His Death	188
For My Father	189
For Abbie Hoffman	190
On Jerry Rubin's Death	192
For John Belushi	193
Red Rose for Huey Newton	194
KPFA at Full Moon	197

Confessional	199
Deep In My Heart	200
For Miranda on Her 40th Birthday	201
Song An Embrace for Chris	202
For Meridel with All Love	203
The Present of Your Presence	205
Mother's Day 1989	207
Song for My Mother	208
Lullaby Blues by Chris Bergman	208
Palestine Petalled	209
Persian Gulf Sonnet	212
Persian Gulf Limericks	212
Thanksgiving Day 1991	215
He Was the "First"	217
Quincentennial Limericks	218
The Next 500 Years	220
Freedom Is A Constant Struggle: July 4, 1992	221
Rodney King and Me	228
Moon Over Mandela	232
Thank You Spike!	234
When Eddie Marshall Plays...	236
Does Santa Believe?	237
Valentine's Day, inspired by Cricket	239
Harvest Time	241
Red Diaper Baby	242
For Anna on Her Batmitzvah	243
Batmitzvah Sonnet for Maia	245
Sonnet to Mark on his 50th Birthday	245
Leaves of Love for Leib	246
Tutsi, Hutu Live in Peace	247
To Irving Fromer on his 80th Birthday	248
Seasonal Greetings	250
Delicious Flan	251
The Redwood Anthem	252
The Great Global Warming Limerick Debate	253
Turtle Island Mother Earth	254
Thirtieth Anniversary of My Mother's Death	255
Mama Mural	257
One More For Chris	258
Anna on Stage	258
On Turning 50	259
Acid Rain Limericks	260
Tessellation Jingle	260
Ode to the Earthworm	261

Penguin Deluxe	261
The Sun is a Star	261
Stability	262
On Sandy Shores	263
Of Time and the River	264
Planetary Verses	266
Brief Ode to Glenn	267
The Plates	268
Fifty Lines for Fifty-Year Olds	271
Working Hands	272
Great Mother Matriarch	273
Children Like Plants	274
Post-Election, November 9, 1994	275
A Few Millennial Appreciations	278
Sonnet for Miranda	280
Mother's Day 1997	280
For Arch Williams	281
For Bernie on His 70th	282
Five Haikus	282
For Frank and Karen	283
On That Bridge	283
Thinking Continually of Mario	284
Mario to Meridel: A Meditation	285
Frère Allen	286
Robert Williams	287
Different Then	288
Silly Sonnet on Poetic Ambition	288
KPFA Limericks	289
I Sing the Radio Eclectic *or* Democracy When?	291
For Kwame Turé	293
Millennial Sonnet	293
Fist of Resistance	294
Ode to a Knee	295
Message to Geronimo	296
March 17	297
Keep the Spirit Alive in the Year '95	297
Sonnet for Anna at 21	298
Another for Anna	298
Madeleine	299
3 July	299
Sonnet for 1999	300
Quick Poem: Computer Desktop	301
Moon Over Rochdale Village	302
Betty's Blues	303

Recipe	305
Dementia	305
Carnelian of Our Christmas Days	306
On Mahealani's Death by Caitlin	
Simpson-Bergman	307
Ending the Year 1998	308
For Anne and Meridel	309
Sweeping Ode to Lisa's Holiday Brooms	310
For the Millennium	311
A Turning Point	313
September 11, 2001	314
Baghdad by the Bay	317
Blair/Bush	317
Wolfie Limericks	318
If Sharon's A Man of Peace	319
Baghdad: Embedded Sonnet	319
Song: O Little Town of Bethlehem	320
Jenin	321
If I Could Paint	322
Closing Prayer	323
Chants Finale	323
End Note	324

I Come and Stand at Every Door
by Nazim Hikmet, revolutionary Turkish poet

I come and stand at every door
But no one hears my silent tread
I knock and yet remain unseen
For I am dead, for I am dead.

I'm only seven though I died
In Hiroshima long ago
I'm seven now as I was then
When children die they do not grow.

My hair was scorched by swirling flame
My eyes grew dim, my eyes grew blind
Death came and turned my bones to dust
And that was scattered by the wind.

I need no fruit, I need no rice
I need no sweet, nor even bread
I ask for nothing for myself
For I am dead, for I am dead.

All that I ask is that for peace
You fight today, you fight today
So that the children of this world
May live and grow and laugh and play.

Acknowledgments

True acknowledgment would be a book in itself—in its modest way this book acknowledges all those whose courage to live life and face its obstacles with humor, wisdom, and tenacity has inspired me:

To my mother Anne, artist, sparkling-eyed wonderful lover of children, reading teacher and proofreader, compassionate, tender and principled, who died tragically of multiple myeloma (a form of bone cancer) when I was in my late teens.

To my father Leibel, utterly brilliant, funny, charming, maddening, romantic, a dedicated and lifelong active revolutionary with extraordinary energy and joie de vivre. Both my parents' spirits naturally sing in every line of mine. I've included a bit of their poetry as well.

To my two wonderful daughters, Anna Thai Binh and Caitlin Poema, who have had to put up with a not-always-so-cheerful and a-little-bit-odd kind of dad, I dedicate these other precious daughters and sons of mine, my poems.

To the rest of my family and its wonderful extensions: my sister Miranda, world muralist, community organizer extraordinaire, revolutionary cultural worker, and my brother Christopher, true soul brother, healer of hearts, great counselor who's been there himself, and fantastic animal person. I treasure their love beyond measure. To Miranda's partner and my fellow poet, Felix Shafer; and Chris' partner Mike Wheeler, fellow mystery fan, both of whom have been oft subjected to my poetic recitals at family gatherings!

To the grandparents I was fortunate to know—grandma Doris ("Dolly") and grandpa Morris, who gave us so much, and gave me a book of world poetry I still treasure. To my father's parents, Sam and Molly, who I never had the chance to know. To my aunts and uncles, cousins near and far, to the intertwining ancestral threads of extended family, all part and parcel of the fabric of these lines.

To the women without whom I would not be who and what I am today, who somehow saw fit, for better and worse, to share the intimacy of daily life with me through various decades:

For my wife, Lisa Caitlin Simpson, Caitlin's mom, whose steady affirming lovelight, compassion, understanding, and poetic soul have helped to give me the strength to carry on and to sustain my creative efforts... my love for her is boundless. I hope that I too, despite many failings, have been there for her as she winds along on her own future pathways, as we walk on together.

To Gayle Markow—we were together during the early seventies through mid-eighties, friends before and since, and spent a year in Cuba together—Anna's caring mom, a dedicated nurse, and spiritual seeker/finder.

To Arlene Eisen—partner and comrade through the passionate, tumultuous, exhilarating, and trying times of the mid- to late-sixties, author and activist whose works include *Women of Vietnam*.

Many poems in this volume were inspired and/or critiqued by these helpmates, as well as other loves and comrades, and by those many women and men whose friendship and mutual respect I treasure, the co-workers and co-conspirators who at one time or another became as family...for, deep in my heart, I do believe, that friendship is the most precious energy of all. My father envisioned a time when "Friendship over Greed and Lust prevails," and I second that emotion! These lines cannot help but also sing out especially for:

Victoria Garvin, who became our new mother when she and my father were married in a "Red Guard" wedding in China, and whose herstory of dedication to the African-American struggle for freedom, the labor movement, Africa, China, and international solidarity is inspiring.

Dorothy Stoffer Broms, my aunt and my mother's closest sister—a sonneteer herself. One of her sonnets is included in this book. A teacher of developmentally disabled children in New York City for many years, Aunt Dorth has more recently graced both Toronto and Berkeley with her presence. She read and commented on an earlier selection of these poems. This book is also dedicated to Dorothy's late husband, Wilbur Broms, my uncle, a superb Irish tenor who was "white-listed" by the New York Met, and whose wise words on culture and revolution resound within me.

Bernard Stoffer, my mother's younger and only brother, who ventured out to the San Francisco Bay Area with my father in the early fifties. Uncle Bernie, whose joie de vivre, warm and friendly energy, and creative versatility continue to amaze me.

Meridel LeSueur, "in my book," one of the greatest people of this century, and one of the most rooted, creative, powerful, and least recognized writers in the world. Meridel has always been one of my most consistent encouragers—a spiritual and familial grand-mother and practical revolutionary—a true worker in words. My poem for Meridel's 90th birthday is but a fragment of my love.

Deborah LeSueur, my aunt and Meridel's daughter, in her own right a talented and accomplished artist and sculptor, a wisewoman who brings out feelings, creates rituals of life and passage, envisions healthier selves and situations. Deborah has always encouraged my creative efforts and was kind enough to read and comment on this collection.

Elsa Knight Thompson, my radio comrade and exemplar, whose experience with the BBC during World War II laid the foundation for her enormous accomplishments in public radio, especially as Public Affairs Director for KPFA-FM from the 1950s through the 1970s. I worked closely with her when I was News Director at KPFA in the late 60s and early 70s. Always controversial, a speaker of truth to power who did not suffer fools gladly, Elsa's social and political dedication were marvelous, her energy astonishing, and her contributions as a journalist and advisor to movements such as Women for Peace, the United Farmworkers, the Black Panther Party, major and mostly still unsung. And for Alexander Hoffmann, a dear friend who I first met as Elsa's longtime sidekick, a brilliant and compassionate human being whose own contributions deserve their own detailed acknowledgment, and who has always encouraged my poetic efforts.

For Joseph Blum, comrade, scholar, working class activist, great photographer, close friend over many years, whose sage advice and love mean much to me. Joe and all the other editors of *The Movement* newspaper also deserve my gratitude for publishing some of my poems during the second half of the 1960s—I was honored to serve on the editorial board of this publication that began as a voice for the Student Non-Violent Coordinating Committee (SNCC) and later also affiliated with Students for a Democratic Society (SDS). *The Movement* became a nationally respected journal that made important analytical and organizing contributions to the movements from which it took its name.

Mark Merin, college roommate at Cornell and close and very generous friend through all the many years since then, crusading attorney and arts patron, legal battler for abortion rights and the Feminist Women's Health Center, and against police brutality. Mark's counsel, encouragement, and generous material support have been instrumental in helping propel me to complete this volume. Cathleen Williams, activist, attorney, and poet, whose encouragement of my efforts should be exceeded by recognition of the beauty of her own...and for Mark and Cathleen's two offspring, Noah and Maia, recipients of several of my stories and poems, and of my love, now on their own ways through the world.

For Claude Marks, dear friend and comrade, who co-produced the early radio programs with me, providing his own special brand of production wisdom, journalistic skills, hands-on and organizational genius, reporter during People's Park, KPFA Production Director, ten years underground, former political prisoner who has been the driving force behind The Freedom Archives. And for others in those early radio years—dedicated prison reporter Mark Schwartz and KPFA stalwart Denny Smithson. For lifelong activist and longtime friend Nancy Barrett, also an early radio collaborator, who was there during some intense political times, and has returned to lend her wisdom and optimism to the Freedom Archives. For Emiliano Echeverria, who sustained the radio program over many years, labored mightily on his own outstanding KPFA productions, and worked with me on programs highlighting struggle and culture, with separate series on Paul Robeson, Pete Seeger, and Langston Hughes.

For Barbara Lubinski, a wise, warm, and generous friend and comrade who read an earlier version of this book, whose own poetry sings out powerful and passionate, who's produced many radio programs, including several we've co-produced featuring children's poetry; for Heber Dreher, a sharply analytical and no-holds-barred talk-show host whose segment was named "Frank Talk,"(the pen name of South African martyr Steven Biko); for community activist, poet, and storyteller Nina Serrano who has produced many unique cultural programs; Kiilu Nyasha, lifelong advocate for political prisoners, and all the others who've given voice with me on the radio waves, over more than 30 years, as part of the KPFA News, The Midnight Flash, The Real Dragon, Nothing Is More Precious Than, and Freedom Is A Constant Struggle.

For Toby Garten, with gratitude for an especially *simpatico* friendship; for Bryan Nichols, whose respect and affection I treasure, and for the other co-workers at the American Academy of Ophthalmology where I toiled and learned about the human eye for half a decade. For Jerry Shapiro, who helped me through a hard time and encouraged me to "write my own story." For Jacqueline Barber (her entire great family!) and Kay Fairwell, who first took on an itinerant half-time editor, and for so many other creative and dedicated co-workers, friends, and comrades—too many to name—at that buzzing beehive of science and math education known as the Lawrence Hall of Science, at the University of California at Berkeley, where I've been happily en-sconced in the Great Explorations in Math and Science (GEMS) program for more than 17 years. Thanks to all GEMS workers and contributors, past and present, to Steve Andrews at the University of California Printing Services, and all the folks there who have helped us with so many projects. And to Colin Hocking, a wonderful Austra-lian friend and co-author of two environmental GEMS guides, who helped get me back into limericks!

To the great cultural exemplars who inspired these poems, artists and activists, poets and prophets: Harriet Tubman—one of the most inspiring human beings who ever lived, Thomas Paine, William Blake. Frederick Douglass, Sojourner Truth, Susan B. Anthony, John Brown, Walt Whitman—the good gay grey poet, Emma Goldman, labor leader Lucy Parsons, socialist Helen Keller, Cuban independence leader and scholar-poet, José Marti, Ho Chi Minh and Mao Tse-tung, both world poets, W.E.B. DuBois—who prophetically said the problem of the twentieth century is the problem of the color line, Paul Robeson—who, as Pete Seeger said, should have been President—or, as Ossie Davis put it when Paul Robeson died, "the tallest tree in our forest has fallen," Langston Hughes—whose rhythmic blues and resistant rhymes sound deep down in my soul, Margaret Walker—chantress of her people, Nicolas Guillen—whose Afro-Cuban chants and rhythms translated his people's music into poetry, and who I had the great good fortune to meet in Havana, Pablo Neruda—whose brilliance, passion, and eloquent love for the natural world create a poetry without parallel, Nazim Hikmet—Turkish Communist poet, whose prison poems, love poems, and epics, make him one of the greatest poets of the 20th century, monumental muralists and artists Diego Rivera, Frida Kahlo, David Alfaro Siqueiros, José Orozco, Kathe Kollwitz, poets and changemakers Roque Dalton, Otto René Castillo, Lu Hsun, Vladimir Mayakovsky, Bertolt Brecht, Mike Quin, Sean O'Casey, Christopher Caudwell, Federico Garcia Lorca, Violetta Parra, Victor Jara, Woody Guthrie, Pete Seeger, Ruby Dee, Ossie Davis, Lorraine Hansberry, James Baldwin, Ralph Ellison, John O. Killens, Tillie Olson, Malvina Reynolds, Sweet Honey in the Rock, Audre Lorde, Phil Ochs, Allen Ginsberg, Gary Snyder, Maya Angelou, Amiri Baraka, Julius Lester, Sonia Sanchez, Nikki Giovanni, Erika Huggins, the late great June Jordan, Joy Harjo, Adrienne Rich, Marge Piercy, Diane di Prima, Judy Grahn, Margaret Randall, Jack Hirschman, John Ross, Susan Griffin, Pat Parker, devorah major, Roberto Vargas, Lawrence Ferlinghetti, Janice Mirikitani—and so many others!

For the sisters and brothers who lit the spark of civil rights and Black Liberation that ignited so much more, for the freedom-riding movement that inspired us all, for Rosa Parks and Fannie Lou Hamer, the Student Non-Violent Coordinating Committee (SNCC), Bob Moses and those trumpeters of Joshua, among them H. Rap Brown (Jamil Abdullah Al-Amin), Stokely Carmichael (Kwame Turé), James Forman, the Deacons for Defense and Justice, Malcolm, Martin, the Black Panther Party, the Black Liberation Army. For the four sweet girls killed in church on Birmingham Sunday, for Chaney, Schwerner, and Goodman, Medgar Evers, Viola Liuzzo, and all victims of Klan violence. For Robert F. Williams, who I knew in China, a courageous advocate of the right of self defense and a lifelong crusader for freedom.

For tender friend Mario Savio, one of the best of us, whose eloquence and profoundly democratic spirit, honesty, and passion will live forever in our hearts. For all of us who marched against or in some way resisted the war against Vietnam and all of Indochina, including SDSers, Vietnam veterans, draft dodgers of all varieties, saboteurs and singers, revolutionaries, clandestine collectives, underground media activists, radicals, peaceniks—for the Vietnamese, Cambodian, and Laotian peoples and for all "Third World" independence movements and insurgencies— Puerto Rico, Palestine, the Philippines, Angola, Guinea-Bissau, Chile, Nicaragua, to name only a few. For the millions of women who struggled for equality, whose consciousness and militance built the resurgent women's liberation movement, for every man who demonstrates practical and consistent feminist understanding and solidarity, and for the current resistance against the vicious attempts to roll back freedoms won, including attacks on the right of reproductive choice. For those who rebelled at Stonewall, who march in San Francisco, for the great pansexual rainbow arc of men and women who have now opened their hearts and closet doors to affirm their sexuality and celebrate love as the millennium arrives. And, as this is published in 2003, for all who marched against the invasion of Iraq.

For the many millions whose dedicated energies crested the worldwide tide of radical change whose spirit shook the 20th century. From high school organizing to the Gray Panthers, from southern Africa to northern Ireland, these movements, so often belittled or mocked, will be seen—when viewed from the vantagepoint of a few hundred years hence—as a major contribution to the foundation of freedom, justice, and peace. For those whose lives call forth the prophecy of Ho Chi Minh who said, "when the prison doors are opened the real dragon will fly out." For all our political prisoners, latter-day heroes and "sheroes"—for the framed representative of the First Peoples, Leonard Peltier; for Black Panther leader Geronimo Ji Jaga (now released); for old friend Marilyn Buck, and for Mumia Abu Jamal, the Afro-American people's journalist on Death Row. It is as Ho wrote:

> See how the rice must suffer under the pestle
> Yet afterward it comes out burnished bright
> The same thing happens to people in this world
> Misfortune's workshop turns them into polished jade.

Finally, for the many I do not name but who have loved, struggled, resisted, created, shared, healed, laughed, cried, agonized, or in some other way worked together alongside me—you know who you are. Please be assured that you are in my heart and your voices and visions have helped me sing these simple songs of freedom.

A Few Words of Poetic Introduction

As well as poems, these lines reflect my growing and changing consciousness over the last half of the 20th century—a century that Meridel Le Sueur has accurately termed the bloodiest century in human history. These lines need to be seen in their historical context—from adolescent awakenings during the post-World War II repression of McCarthyism through development of the African-American civil rights and liberation movements, the struggle against the war in Vietnam and Indochina, and the resurgence of movements for radical change inside the United States.

Continuing past that high point of optimism and collective spirit, these poems must also reflect the murderous splintering of these movements, the ascendancy of the most backward of the aristocratic classes, the awareness by the millions who succeeded in ending the war in Indochina that the revolutionary transformations they had once thought so probable and imminent were not to come to pass in the way that anyone had foreseen.

There is an overarching socio-political lesson that emerges for me from these times, and that is, as Chairman Mao put it, that "the people and the people alone are the true makers of history." The mass nature of social change asserts itself again and again.

Combined with this social lesson is another, more personal truth, again articulated by Mao Tse-tung (echoing Confucius and countless others) when he said, "before you can change the world, you must first change yourself." Personal transformations of many kinds not envisioned by the Chairman have certainly been the name of the game in recent decades!

These poems reflect my life passage through the second half of the past century. In some cases I have included notes to situate a poem historically, or to comment on its evolution (and my own) over time. They are roughly but not precisely chronological, after the introductory section. From this body of work, you can create your own images and draw your own conclusions about pathways and struggles of my spirit as I became more myself over time, as my humanhood grows and my throat opens to sing. While this collection represents more than the tip of the iceberg, it is a selection. Numerous additional poems fill my files— birthday odes, hundreds of radio scripts often with poetry, plays, puppet shows, stories for children. I've written many poems for young people on science and math topics, published by the Lawrence Hall of Science in Berkeley, where I am Associate Director of the Great Explorations in Math and Science (GEMS) curriculum series. Some of these math and science poems are included in this collection.

As you will see, many of these poems were written in the heat and passion of social involvement and were not sculpted to the finely-chiseled degree demanded by the accomplished poets of our age. Other odes are in the realm of "occasional poetry," written for a birthday, an anniversary, a memorial. Some may read like greeting cards, or be seen as overly sentimental, romantic, polemical, Pollyannish—nonetheless many have been appreciated in their own time and place. Some may call them doggerel (or as we joke in our cat-rich household—"catterel.") I recognize some of their limitations and my own lack of discipline, but make no apologies for the messages they seek to broadcast. I salute William Topaz McGonagall, poet of Dundee, widely hailed as the writer of the worst poetry in the English language! A self-educated handloom weaver, his poetry blossomed in 1877, beginning a 25-year career of writing and reciting, humorously delighting audiences with wildly stretched rhymes across Scotland and beyond.

I too celebrate the heart of rhyme in my work—it is of course a major attribute of songs, some great poetry, and many famous speeches, from Shakespeare to Malcolm X, William Blake to Allen Ginsberg. In particular, the works of Langston Hughes and Maya Angelou ring with rhyme (and much more)! Rhyme is intrinsic to the blues—that powerful and original poetic form that is one of the greatest contributions of Afro-American artists to world culture. In its most intricate and cleverly internal forms, rhyme is a compelling attribute of rap and hip hop—the "boom poetic." The poem "My Lifelong Love Affair" speaks for itself. This book was almost called "A Rhyme in Time," or "A Rhymin' Time." Each day we see the power of rhyme to move people, from inane commercials to sublime lyrics. I'll say it again—rhyme is key to the power of the blues, and the blues my friends is what it's all about!

Many of these poems are chants and incantations, meant to be "out-spoken," read out loud with the variety of rhythms and intonations in the human voice. Some of the poems stem directly from my years of radio broadcasting. Poetry, it's been said, is a heightened form of ordinary speech. Perhaps at its most spiritual and authen-tic, poetry arrives as if a voice is speaking through the poet—the poet a transmission mode through which meanings emerge. It is to be profoundly celebrated when a genuine spark of universal inspiration succeeds in speaking through the poet, when a collec-tive spirit is expressed, a group feeling resonated, an experience shared, insight gained, love expressed, goddesses celebrated!

These poems express my love of life, for all its pain and sorrow. They are dedicated to the cause of Justice, without which there cannot be Peace. They trace a pathway I've travelled on within and through our times. They also represent an internal journey, reflect-ing facets of that intricate gemstone we call personality, different sides of myself. They are the songs of my soul, the chants of a lifetime. With that, they are in your hands.

Start, She Said

Start
She said
Anywhere
Start
With the ocean
Crashing on the shore!

Opening Invocation

Muse of my soul
Summon up once more
The child's first cry
Give it one more try—

Muse of our times
Gift me the rhymes
To sing my heart
To fashion art

Red bowl of clay
Blue sky above
May Justice and Peace
Meet lines of Love.

Just Pour It Out...

Meridel Le Sueur was one of the 20th century's great people's writers, a spirit and soul for the ages. These phrases from one of Meridel's letters to me shine as her preface to these poems... she will always be sitting in the same room with me.

It was just about the loveliest thing in the world to receive this wonderful rose at the beginning of our journey and your beautiful poem. It was strange this rose was enormous shaped like a vase and deep red and large. I carried it every day and it was so sensitive it would loosen and move outward when it was warm and hit by light and then close up at night. It had its stem in a little glass vase and it was visible for over a week and I now have it pressed. It seemed and was a living articulation and I shall always remember it as a red force then it opened into a bowl of blood given as roses do its entire circle of energy...entirely wonderfull red and open. I have come here to bring in my crop before frost. I really have three large remarks I want to make—three symphonies...I do want to do it.

Dearest Lincoln—There has been some speed and distance in all the happenings. I pray for your life and work...I am going to come there just to somehow sit quietly in the same room with you. Just pour it out never mind being a commodity or being seen. All our thoughts and images are needed and give light...I love you...

Meridel

A Korean Baby

A Korean baby, newly born, lies dead in the bitter snow-
Not ever to suckle, never to kick his little feet,
Never to smile into his mother's eyes.
Korean mother, my sister across the distant sea,
We shall avenge your nameless baby, unfulfilled, deprived,
Never to be replaced
No matter how many future children may be born.
We will not let the world forget him —
Like Lidice, like Sacco and Vanzetti and the Jewish children
Murdered by the fascists,
Your son too is numbered in our hearts —
We shall avenge him.

> Anne Lucille Stoffer Bergman, my mother,
> during the Korean war, 1952

Frustration

To live from day to day is not enough,
And yet our means are scarce. Perhaps that's all
We can encompass while the seas are rough.
Perhaps we can't contend— must ride the squall.
To live from day to day — is that our force,
Our lonely weapon when we can't unite?
We throttle anger as we shed remorse;
We live a week, a year, and gather might.

Guerrilla-like we hide our giant hate,
Take refuge in a silence, forest dark;
We light another cigarette and wait,
Hold back the arrow though we see the mark.
Will we know when to answer to alarm?
Will we remember how to lift an arm?

> Leibel Bergman, my father, during the
> Cuban missile crisis, 1962

Invocation for a Green Thumb
(dedicated to my pre-trainable children)

The children who "can't be taught" are those I teach.
Exploring step by minute step the way
To lead them to some light, to help them reach
The highest step they can. Thus every day
Must be a day of living striving growth.
Their feeble roots need tending. I am loath
To any longer leave to sad decay
Children who can be coaxed to learn and play.

There is a rare delight that gardeners find
Who nurture fragilest plants to precious bloom
A special pleasure like to one on whom
Falls the most delicate and arduous kind
Of labor with these little ones who will
Reach upward toward the sun when touched with skill.

by Dorothy Jo Stoffer Broms
New York City, May 2, 1960

Note: As mentioned in the Acknowledgments, my mother's
sister Dorothy, the author of this sonnet, was for many years
an outstanding teacher of developmentally disabled children
in New York City. She now spends her time in both Toronto
and Berkeley. Later poems in this book are dedicated to
Dorothy and her late husband, Wilbur Broms. Dorothy has
written many sonnets over the years and several powerful
poems about her teaching experience and the nuclear
nightmare. She has much wisdom and a sparkling sense of
humor and word play—for example, her four syllable
version of her full name—Do Jo Sto Bro! I chose the poem
above to represent her work and because the metaphor
connects so strongly with my mother, who loved plants and
children too. Dorothy in her eighties has self-published her
poetry (with my computer assistance) in a collection called
Sonnets and Some Songs.

Great Profligate Poet

O may my heart's truth
Still be sung
> — Dylan Thomas
> Poem in October

Great profligate poet
Born like me
On October 27th
When I turned 50
You would have been 80
Did your bleached bones
Beat the coffin walls
In celebration?
Reading your
Collected poems
I humbly bow and listen
To the rush of truth
The soar of song
Open wide my ears
To hear the aching
Chorus of your genius.

Rip Van Winkle

(a very early childhood poem, maybe 1950, 6 years old)

When Rip Van Winkle came home one night,
All the stars were shining bright,
His wife was in a very good mood,
She made him go out and hunt some food.
Now Rip, he met some little men,
Not too many, about nine or ten,
They gave him some whiskey and beers,
And then he slept for twenty years.
He grew a beard so very far
It was almost as long as our car.
He came home it was 1788.
He met his daughter and son—
He told them the whole story
As he saw Old Glory wave above.

Introducing the Poet

My name is Lincoln Bergman
From Herstory I come
I bathed in primal ocean
'Twas in the year of None

My name is Lincoln Bergman
From History I come
I crawled the rock of ages
'Twas in the year of One

I crawled the rock of ages
To wish my dreams come true
To harvest all my crops
'Twas in the year of Two

To harvest all my crops
I loved and danced so free
Wheat and rice and corn
'Twas in the year of Three

I loved and sometimes learned
I marched against the war
I wrote a thousand poems
'Twas in the year of Four

I spoke a thousand poems
Made broadcasts taped and live
For freedom and for peace
'Twas in the year of Five

I played a thousand games
And laughed at all the tricks
Of darling daughters two
'Twas in the year of Six

I worked and worked and worked
But rarely did bread leaven
The money slipped right through
'Twas in the year of Seven.

Sad story of my life
Too little and too late
Confronted by mortality
'Twas in the year of Eight.

Yet days when we make love
Create a world so fine
Conjoining energies
'Twas in the year of Nine.

And so my story goes
From now till way back when
My heart is in my hands
For 'tis the year of Ten.

My Lifelong Love Affair

I've had a lifelong love affair
With something always in a pair
So connected as to be
A single mingled melody
A love so strong
A love so long
A love so certain and so true
A love that's always old and new
A love that sings
A love that brings
A sweet release
A sense of peace
A love imbibed in mother's milk
That's warm as sun and smooth as silk
A love passed on by father's hand
A love that helps me understand
A love that fills with poetry
A love of you, a love of me
An intimate, passionate love affair
As natural as breathing air
Withstanding all the winds of time
My lifelong love affair with rhyme!

Starting Out Again Tonight

Starting out again tonight from that time of tragedy
The conclusion was inescapable
The pain irremediable...

Starting again from that day in the desert
When I heard from a distance that my mother had died
Of multiple myeloma, a form of bone cancer...

My father's sad sad voice telling me...
Thirty-one years ago exactly
As I return again to that moment I remember how
The tears flowed; it had snowed the night before
Desert snow at Deep Springs salted by tears
Of which there can never be enough...

The love my sister and brother and I share
Has so much of my mother's love in it
The love I have to give to those who care for me
Reflects and carries on her love for children and beauty
We were all so deeply deeply touched by
Her compassionate and special radiance...

Starting from this moment
May that ocean of sorrow
Again give birth to life—
May single- and multi-celled organisms
Creep up the beach of my soul to consciousness
Fashion purpose, emerge with life-force energy,
Evolve with animal-human indigenuity
To at last reach Justice, which is the gate to Peace.

Starting from this moment
May my own sense of being part
Of the wondrous webs of nature's warp and woof
Sustain and nourish me and all whom I hold dear

Starting from this moment
May my love of writing
Present you, dear reader, with these
Songs of my soul.

Century Plant

A century of our life passes
Lives and battles lost and won
A century of our strife passes
One-hundred times around the Sun
One hundred years of struggle
One hundred revolutions of
The planet Earth around the Sun
What is to be done?
A century of blood
What can possibly be done?

The century plant,
Legend has it,
Only blooms once in a hundred years...

Actually I'm told, it's more like every thirty years,
Depending on the climate
Cyclical, like the decades perhaps,
From the 30s, to the 60s, to the 90s,
Eras of rebellion and change blossoming
Times of conservative retreat between
How desperately it seems human beings
Seek to extract some larger meaning
From the passage of the years
The ebb and flow of human tidal glue
Upon this spinning orb of greenish-blue

Dear reader of my heart and mind and soul
I leave the interpretation up to you
The putting together of the puzzle in your hands
You the detective; you to solve the mystery.
I only spin my web in lines of poetry
As a recorder of this bloodiest century
Bringing the events to your attention
Leaving the main things to you.

Like wondrous Walt Whitman
Cataloguing the century
Providing brief glances
Shy, like those of young love,
Like Marti's wounded fawn,
Seeking refuge in the forest,
Outlining the sad and glorious century
In ways we never learned in school.

I do not expect you to agree with me
Only that you listen with the same respect
I would accord you
Only that you hear me out
Then use your own fine brain
To separate the wheat from chaff
Enjoy a rhyme, let loose a laugh.

I only ask that you apply
Your independent thinking skills
To the vast and fiery riddles of our century
That you review our bloody passage
With wise eyes turned toward century to come

So at last this Earth may bloom
Our race face forward, not meet doom,
Our precious kernels of creation
Not destroyed by exploitation
Sweet flowers of our evolution
Not be crushed by brute pollution—

Ask you to pause and think a while
Of that bright day when "Earth shall smile."

The Frameups Shall Cease

When Ethel and Julius Rosenberg died
It was because the bosses had lied
Ethel and Julius false would not tell
As for the bosses, they can go to hell.

Ethel and Julius died in the electric chair
But the bosses didn't seem to care
When they died they gave new spirit to us
If we don't have peace the world will bust.

As long as the dove of peace shall fly
The thought of peace shall never die
Before very long we shall have peace
Then all the frameups shall cease.   1953

Note: This, I am proud to say, was my first published poem, appearing in the Letters section of the national newspaper of the Communist Party, the Daily Worker. Nine years old, I was, like every child of progressive parents, deeply traumatized by the execution of the Rosenbergs. It could have been my parents dragged away and framed on fabricated charges, murdered by anti-Communist hysteria. As it was, the FBI harassed my parents, their comrades and families on their jobs, knocked on our door, and, in addition to numerous FBI-inspired job losses, phone taps, and other surveillance, my father was charged with aiding and abetting a fugitive, an African-American woman, Eunice Caldwell, who was charged with a state loyalty oath violation. Charges against my father were eventually dropped, though the publicity made it even more difficult to find work, contributing to his move in 1952 to San Francisco. The rest of the family followed a year later. During his absence, I wrote him many letters from my sincere 7-year-old self, and one of them was a poem about "Sam Sam, the Swingin' Man." He used it to come up with the *nom de guerre/de plume* he used in publishing many poems during those repressive years and later—Sam Swing. My father wrote several published poems in honor of the Rosenbergs and both my parents and thousands of others around the country worked tirelessly on their behalf. My mother was one of the leading signature gatherers in the mass petition campaigns to prevent their execution. There was something in my mother's spirit, in her eyes and smile, that inspired trust and confidence. I can imagine her calmly informing a not-very-political Minnesota middle-aged couple concerning the facts of the case, her reasonableness persuasive, shining with the quiet fire of her spirit. The two sons of the

Rosenbergs have established a foundation that helps children of political prisoners and those martyred in the struggle for human freedom. For years in my study I stared at a photograph of a wonderful batik that the artist Lisa Kokin made for the Rosenbergs. I told my daughters the tragic story with great emotion, even as I also sang them to sleep with, sure, lots of lullabies and pop songs, but also "Joe Hill." Later we sang along with Holly Near and Ronnie Gilbert singing that powerful song to Sacco and Vanzetti, "Their Own Two Hands."

With the corrupt crumbling of the Soviet Union, there have been reports that the Rosenbergs were "guilty," according to supposed files made public in Moscow. True, they, like many thousands of others, like my father and mother, supported in various ways and/or had personal contacts with the Soviet Union and Eastern Europe through their membership in the Communist Party. But how the media and even sincere historians can swallow these new reports hook, line, and sinker is beyond me, particularly when it has been known for years that there were really no atomic secrets to be stolen. The greatest play of our era, *Angels in America*, brings in the Rosenberg case and the bizarre persona and career of Roy Cohn and understands the profound and continuing cultural consequences. For the historical record, not out of sentimentality (though that is evident) I am convinced of their essential innocence and courage beyond all words.

One of my father's poems foresaw a day when we would "walk down Rosenberg Street to Rosenberg Square." Ethel Rosenberg's poems and letters echo deep down in my soul. Even on Death Row she envisioned a time of justice and peace—saying that "the Earth shall smile," a line I borrowed in ending the poem on page 26. My uncle Wilbur Broms sang one of her poems set to music: "... Work and build my sons, and build, a monument to hope and joy, to human worth, to faith we kept, for you, my sons, for you..." Morton Sobell served 30 years on Alcatraz in connection with the case. My father wrote: "His crime was friendship so he walked in stone." In all the intervening years I've wished my childhood poetic predictions might prove prophetic, but, just take a look around—the frameups have not ceased.

Free Mumia Abu Jamal
Free Marilyn Buck
Bring Assata Shakur Home Free
Free Leonard Peltier
Freedom for all political prisoners!

Spectator (1961)

Near the park baseball field
An old twisted tree
Creaks in the wind.

A young boy sits in the stands
Next to him his glove
With a baseball in it
And a portable radio.

He watches the practice grounders
Sometimes he fingers
The stitches on the clean white ball.

He comes here every day,
No conversationalist
He can only listen
To the creaking of the tree.

Fillmore Temple (1961)

Hand in hand the couple stood
Beneath the colored arc of light
That framed the altar.

Above them stood two men
One spoke, translating the words
The other sang.

They blessed this couple
The cantor's outstretched hands
Sealed their promise.

Across the street the liquor store
Was surrounded by talking men
One singing, all out of work.

The synagogue was stone between
The high wooden houses
Whose windows had no windowshades.

From one of the windows a Negro woman
In her bathrobe looked down
Toward the bus stop at a waiting boy
And he looked up.

Synagogue in Mourning   1962

The rhythmic
Chant. Almost
A melody
A weekly
Panegyric.

He reads those
Dead from the
Congregation:
Libation.
The list goes:

Bernstein, good
Father. Gold-
Farb, first world war,
Many more.
All men stood

And slowly
Sadly said
Kaddish, the death
Prayer, breath
Came harshly

Grief is wild—
The cantor
Alone. His cry
Clear as the eye
Of a child.

Cattle Ranch Operation   *Deep Springs, California 1962*

He slit the stomach expertly,
    then reached inside to feel
        the little legs, the half-formed hooves.
He pulled it out
    and cradled it, but it was dead.
        He said: "Take it to the dump,
So the mother will not know."
    The whole community
        watched the operation.
The cowboy's wife
    said she thought it wrong
        for her daughter to see
That sex and motherhood could mean
    this dusty Caesarean.
        but the cowboy's daughter
Sneaked out of the house
    and 10 years old
        red hair blue eyes
Sat upon the fence
    and watched with all of us.
        He sewed the wound
Back up and gave us instructions
    to keep the mother
        separated so other cows
Would not butt into her
    and open up the wound again.
        We listened well
We knew this would only be the first time—
    Last year some bulls
        had raging
Broken through a fence
    into a pen of heifers
        too young to be bred
And dead
    so small and glistening wet
        with half-formed hooves
Stillborn
    the tiny victim
        of last summer's lust
Untimely ripped
    so small and wet
        and thrown into the dust.

Deep Springs Revisited

Deep springs eternal in my human breast
South meets North where East greets West
Compass of my battered soul
Beneath the sky's inverted bowl
Underground fresh waters run
Deep springs emerging to the Sun
Serene within my aching heart
Pulsing start of every art
Completing the circle, shaping the square
Bringing forth Hope from the Rock of Despair.

    He wandered 'round the desert sands
    Breaking free of mind-forged bands
    Thinking he'd go to any lengths
    To "go down into our land and find the strengths"
    So said her strong prophetic voice
    He made then a conscious choice
    No matter what the fates may send
    To wend his way 'round every bend
    Past all the tragedy and strife —
    To walk upon the Path of Life!!!

For stimulating intellect
The mind is worthy of respect
But brighter in the firmament
Emotional enlightenment
The seasons come and then they go
In ebb and flow, for lo—
Winter at last is over and done
Snow melts in shining of the Sun
Eggs crack to hatch in cradle-nest
South meets North where East greets West
Deep springs eternal in my human breast.

Note: I attended Deep Springs Junior College, a working cattle ranch and noted liberal arts college, from 1961–4. Deep Springs is unique—isolated in the California mountain desert, two valleys up from Death Valley, with 20 male students and 5 professors. An effort toward the end of the 20th century to make the school coeducational unfortunately failed. Deep Springs is a special place and had a profound impact on me. Several friendships made there have been important and lasting. Special places in my heart for Dick Broadhead (a poem on his untimely death appears later in this book), Dr. Philip Craven, who was there for me at Deep Springs taking a stand against anti-Semitism and who further demonstrated his friendship courageously. Other "Deep Springers" have been there for me as well; there is a strong bond created in the desert. I remember Condit Brewer Van Arsdall III, a wonderful friend from Kentucky who was killed in his 20s trying to rescue his baby in an ocean boating tragedy, and David Mossner, a gentle and poetic younger student who, a few years after he left Deep Springs, was killed in Vietnam. I wrote many poems and autobiographical sketches at Deep Springs, but include here only Cattle Ranch Operation and Deep Springs Revisited, written during a reunion visit to the valley in Spring 1984.

My mother died when I was at Deep Springs—I have never forgotten the kindness and generosity of the entire group of students and staff there—it moved me immensely, gave me a powerful sense of the best in all of us, comforted me and my family for this inexpressible loss. And, many years later, It was a Deep Springer and great practitioner of family medicine, Dr. David Werdegar, who, as Acting Public Health Director of San Francisco, helped me find a place for my father during his brilliant and difficult final illnesses.

Completing the circle, shaping the square
Bringing forth Hope from the Rock of Despair

For Walt Whitman

This I know —

As the eagle its nest, as the river its bed,
As the blood its heart —
This I know:

Clear as the dawn is clear,
Clear as the eye of a child,
I see all the sweet singers to come.

Far, far forward I see them; beyond my sight I see them;
At the feet of Walt I see them.

Pondering his powerful visions,
Savoring his warmth and his love,
Nourishing at his harsh and soft speech
I see them.

I see their firm grasp of his themes, and I see how they
magnify his themes,
And I see the new themes that are the daughters and sons
of his themes.

I hear them speak with his voice,
And I hear them speak with all voices, and with new voices;
And the day I see and hear them,
The sweet singers, the children of Walt,
That day is a world to delight in.

For he is singular among the American,
Unique between the oceans,
The solitaire of our seed
To stand with those very few of the very greatest

Poets of the World.

Note: Assistance from my father with a term paper on Walt
Whitman resulted in this collaborative poem, with my father
taking the lead and both of us seeking to spin off from
Whitman's own style, with its King James Bible-like rising
repetitions and prophetic voice, as in Whitman's own "Poets
to Come." The paper was submitted in various forms for
several high school and college English classes. Thanks Pa!

Mind on Freedom to Tracy Sims

Come on Tracy, tell them, make them see
Those people on the bus and on the street
Trudging weary home from work
Call out to them, their ears seem closed
Maybe once the truth has been disclosed
Their fight to get things right will set them free.

Yeh, they've seen injustice before
They seem to shruggingly accept it
"You can't fight City Hall,"
But come on Tracy show them
No matter how many sophistries combine
And wools are pulled,
Ain't gonna let nobody turn us round
And show the students too
Cynicism makes things worse
Belief can get things done
And Tracy show them now!
I'm gonna walk, walk, gonna talk, talk, gonna walk walk
With my mind on Freedom.

"Hey, you guys, come 'ere—block the doors!
That's it, block the doors, fill the floor, more! more!
Are ya ready to go to jail for what ya believe in?
Are ya ready to go to jail for what ya believe in?"

And say it to them calm and reasoned too
Wake them up, block the doors, and then
Tracy, linked arm in arm with you,
We'll all be able to walk on through!

Note: Tracy Sims was a very young African-American
woman who rose to leadership of the civil rights struggle in
San Francisco. She was an inspiring and gifted leader and
became a close friend of my sister and brother. There were a
number of leaders and organizations involved in victorious
and unified battles of the early 1960s to desegregate employ-
ment in San Francisco businesses—hotels, restaurants, auto
row. Those were splendid struggle-filled days, reminiscent
of that wonderful Charles White lithograph of a multiracial
marching demonstration entitled "Walk Along Together," a

print of which is a family treasure my sister has on her wall. The way leadership is thrust on people is a complex phenomenon, the sudden pressures and media manipulations an extreme hazard. I think immediately of Tracy Sims, of Mario Savio at Berkeley, of SNCC, Black Panther, and SDS leaders, and so many others who rose to the occasion as best they could. At that moment in San Francisco Tracy Sims represented the crest of the wave, the exemplar of what we stood for, a voice of certainty, courage, humor, resistance, victory. I was arrested—with more than 900 others—and later served 30 days in jail, for a sit-in blocking the doors of the Sheraton Palace Hotel. We linked arms and passively resisted, making it difficult for police to separate us. Me and a tall Black man named Irvin happened to be next to each other—we held together and they tried to charge us with resisting arrest, with the arresting officer later saying of me, "He looks thin, but he's wiry." We were all charged with disturbing the peace and tried in groups of ten. Many were acquitted. My group, ably defended by none other than Terrence Hallinan, now San Francisco's District Attorney, had the misfortune to draw a judge named Elton Lawless. He was, and we got 30 days, the maximum. "Ain't a scared of your jails cause I want my freedom, I want my freedom, I want my freedom now…" Tracy, wherever you are—know that you are remembered with love and respect.

Orange Apricot Brandy

—The land is a mother that never dies
                           Maori saying

Her wallpaper,
Yellowing, flowers
For final hours;
No escapers

From cancer. A quart
Next to a flowerpot—
Warm brandy, apricot
The only comfort.

                           1963

An Old Riddle

As I was going to Cornell:

I met a gambler dressed in rags
An old man who'd lost his luggage tags
And at Salt Lake a cold rain fell
As I was going to Cornell:

I thought of what I'd left behind
Her voice in song ran through my mind
And a sadness rose I could not quell
As I was going to Cornell:

I sat with a woman whose son had just died
Heard a baby as it laughed and cried
I tossed through Greyhound nights of hell,
As I was going to Cornell.

Rags, love, death, hell—
Why am I going to Cornell?

                           1964

Ithaca Graveyard

A walk downhill past the weekend couples
Who pause to kiss, down from the university
To the fabled graveyard, where, it is said
A girl was once found roaring drunk
Clad only in her underpants.

Such a walk downhill even if during the day
Might well supply some sights worth mention,
These were his thoughts as down he walked
Into the graveyard where his first sight was
The pine trees, and below their green and
The bare branches of the others, he saw a

Trampled can of beer on the slope.
He would have liked it to have an inscription
Like the monuments, that told him the story
Of its being there, but all it said was Schlitz,
And the foot or fist that twisted it had
Long since gone. Long since gone dead mother.

For this was not the first time he had taken
This walk downhill from his study desk, once
He had taken this walk with a girl who, for
Reasons that she couldn't fully explain had
Protested his walking on the burial mounds,
Out of respect. He had answered that the grass
Grew there, he thought it only right that living
Feet should also wander, grow, upon the dead.

Mother you are buried far away and I have never
Visited since the day when all of us threw the
Soil you loved, the soil from which your flowers
Grew, were watered, flowered, upon the casket.
But on this day of rainclouds in the sky, this
Day when feet are drawn to death, I think of you.

One monument had fallen, had redug into the earth
So that the name could no longer be read, and on
One he read the name and year of 1812, a girl
Aged two years, ten months, two days; he thought
Of her as smiling, blue-eyed blond, in a cotton
Dress of blue with white polka-dots, and little feet.

And he remembered the talk of when you are an old
Lady in a black dress, we'll take care of you and
Mother then you smiled but we never saw that day.
And he remembered how near the end she had wanted
To once more hold a baby in her arms, but there
Were no grandchildren then and they can never know her.

There were some tiny stones, he reasoned that
The family had not had much resource, but saw
Them stand against the larger almost oriental
Tombs built into the lower hillside,
And he remembered when he was a little boy.

How whenever he was in a car that passed
A graveyard, even if everyone was talking,
He would silently lower his head at this
Thing which was so unknown but seemed so
Meaningful. Today he saw the stumps of
Trees cut off around the graveyard, and
The Christmas wreaths and flowerpots that
Had been placed there after death.

Other graveyards came to mind, the one
Much further out from Ithaca where he
Had walked with another girl to ease her
Sadness, the loss of her mother, her doubts
About herself and world. They walked and
Turned down the cemetery path at night and
Darkness made each step an adventure, there
Was the fear that with each step would be
An open pit, a wall preventing them from
Going deeper, but then the night became more
Clear and they sat on monuments or grass
And talked, as he walked over to a white
High stone gravemarker to urinate. Suddenly
They heard a siren, growing louder louder
And immediately into their minds that old
Spectre of destruction (everyone curl up
under their desks) raised itself and it went
On and so they talked but then it passed.
Was it the testing that had caused that
Bone-breaking cancer mother that you suffered?

He walked on and heard the thunder,
The day she died, he far away, it had snowed,
That snow merged with falling faintly Joyce
The Dead, and he had heard a lecture on the
Theatre of the Absurd and seen a film of
Himself acting Estragon in Waiting for Godot.
His father called and then he thought,
Remembered his mother's voice a few weeks
Earlier—I should have known that was her goodbye.

Later he would see the notebook that she kept
During those last days, "She whom the gods
Would destroy, they would first make happy,"
Would remember the family at the grave and
Father's words— "because she had so much
Courage, let's all of us have a little bit,"
And he would see, on a torn page, her artistic
Script—to my beloved children I bequeath
All of myself that is in them.

Then it had snowed, in Ithaca it lightly rains
And all things are seen with that same reverence
That once was felt when passing graveyards, and
To the poem, all poems, the love I'm soon to know,
All loves, the graveyards of memory and those in
Ithaca, the pine trees and the leafless ones,
The beer bottles and the drunken naked girls,
To all of these dead mother I bequeath
All of myself that is in you, and all of me
To children you will never see who I must
Gently firmly father, and to those tiny
Monuments that stand against the larger tombs.

He turned around wet in the falling rain
And quietly began to climb the hill once more
Past the trees, the dormitories, and on.

Ithaca, New York, 1965

To Paul and Vietnam Protest at Cornell

And so we find ourselves
    among the dirty pots
Scrubbing at the doubts
    which seem to be burned in
Yet still we scrub.

Going at it differently
    but trying to understand the other's way
In order to understand ourselves.
    In the same way, I can wash them for you now and then
Because wherever you are you're also doing
    Finding out something for me too.

Without these doubts, where
Would we be, could you
Still be able to lead and at
The same time learn
And hold on to a warmth
That no matter how superficial you may think it
Is nowadays so rare, so good, that it demands a poem
That it commands a certain brotherhood?

Sing sometimes man, a way to let it go
And at the same time a way to build
From that limbo where most of us
Are caught. The blues are sung
Sometimes this makes the sadness pass away.

'Cause in the blues, or on the picket line
Somewhere there's hope. My burden's so heavy,
I can hardly see, seems like everybody is down
On me, and that's all right, I don't worry
Oh there will be a better day.

I know that's just words, bullshit, just hopes
Just someday someday someday we shall.
What about tomorrow? At least today today today
Long old lonesome time—today we are not
Afraid, or so we sing.

So sing, with all that worry,
What tomorrow we can't know,
But part of it is forecast by our
Scrubbing of today, and though the
Ways we go will be our own, may be
Dead ends, down many roads, how
Many roads, though all of this is so;
The sometime strength and partial
Understanding build a memory to line
Those roads, and twisting turning
Searching parting scrubbing doubting,
Will help them lead somewhere.

Note: I was at Cornell University for a year in 1964/65. There I
met Arlene Eisen, who I was later to marry. I met some wonder-
ful friends and lived in a place called Telluride House, a stimu-
lating intellectual atmosphere with full scholarship, room and
board. My first roommate was Mark Merin, now a Sacramento
attorney, and we've remained close over the years—later in this
collection there is a sonnet for him. A brilliant graduate student
from India named Gayatri Chakravorty, now a world feminist/
anti-imperial theoretician, was in the room just under mine.
While I was there "the House" hosted people like longterm
resident Frances Perkins, the first woman cabinet member
(Secretary of Labor in the Roosevelt Administration), and
visitors like Amiri Baraka (then called Leroi Jones), Timothy
Leary, Herbert Marcuse, and other scholars, politicians, artists,
and poets. Also there was arch-reactionary professor Allan
Bloom, a Svengali who gathered a small group of disciples
around him, among them Paul Wolfowitz, current Deputy
Secretary of Defense, who never recovered from the elitist spell,
and has become a leading "neo-con" and war criminal (see page
318). But there also, in the kitchen, when the crew who had to
work their way through college by washing dishes at Telluride
did massive dinner cleanup, I'd go back, shoot the shit, and help
out Paul Epstein, a wonderful guy who became a progressive,
activist doctor. He and I were both active in the new Students for
a Democratic Society (SDS) chapter that started on campus that
year. An SDS campus traveller, Jeff Segal (later one of the
Oakland 7) helped stir things up, and, with leadership from
Arlene, the Cornell chapter grew. We rolled down to Washington
DC in April 1965—one of the first big marches against the war in
Vietnam, more than 25,000 of us, hearing Paul Potter, President
of SDS at the time, declare: "We must name the system, analyze
it, change it!" Paul died of cancer some years ago—that speech is
one of the most honest and powerful I ever heard. The cherry
blossoms were enlightening Washington; our prophetic spirits
were helping start what would become a movement of millions
against the war in Vietnam and all of Indochina. Like the
rhythms of the poem to Paul Epstein, the antiwar movement
sprang and sang out of the civil rights movement, sprouted in
the soil made ready by the freedom wave then on the rise.

Acropolitic Sunset   for Arlene

We walk today a narrow street,
And wind a sacred hill,
Past shattered marble, buried deep,
For as ye sow, so shall ye reap,
We walk to worship at Athena's feet.

We lovers walk a narrow street,
And wind a sacred hill,
Past theatre—to laugh, to weep,
Carytides still find no sleep,
Nor is it sleep the lovers seek.

So there the marble stood.
And yet, was not until the sunset
That the shattered marble meant,
Was not until the sunset
That the streaming light
Lay on the dying Parthenon
So that the sacred marble shone,
Carytides were not alone.
Was not until the sunset that we saw
New meaning reconstruct the shattered stone.

New meaning as the setting sun was gold
True gold, not modern Croesus owned,
Sad searching light that lay upon
The history of modern Greece
Brave mariners missed the golden fleece
Sad light upon a vicious Asian war,
And with the gold, a violet glow
Laid bare all inner valleys of despair.
No wonder that we sometimes find
It just to see the shattered world below
With only thoughts of sunset in our minds.

Now sinking still—sun touching mountains
Softly, with a Sistine Chapel touch,
To soon become a thin gold crown
And after final struggle, life or death,
Crowns falling and the epic struggle done.
Great lingering beauty in the afterglow—
Clear lines shimmer in complexity of twilight,
Until the total darkness swallows all our sight.
As, finally, our day, like theirs, is gone—
Another sunset on another Parthenon.

The East is Red

Note: The next poem was one of more than 20 published in a book I wrote, *The East Is Red*, that summarized the history of the Chinese Revolution in verse, with each major event also depicted as a paper cut print created by artists from a people's commune. The book, published by China Books and People's Press, designed by a great artist, Frank Cieciorka, was written a few years after I returned from one year working in the People's Republic of China during 1965 and 1966. I taught college students my own age (20 and 21) as a "foreign expert" at the Institute for International Relations in what was then Peking, now Beijing. While U.S. citizens were not supposed to travel to China in those times, I went with my father and brother, thanks to my father's revolutionary credentials. I was astounded by the sheer numbers of people, the extraordinary depth of Chinese civilization, the level of social organization, the authentic revolutionary spirit of that time, the friendship and energy of my students, the beauty and diversity of the natural landscape. While the word for the United States in Chinese means "beautiful country," China too is absolutely breathtaking. We got to know a unique group of other North Americans already there, including the famous journalist Anna Louise Strong, as well as revolutionaries and adventurers from around the world. I met Chou en Lai. I witnessed the start, but only the start, of the Cultural Revolution. My eyes were also opened to the world, as we lived in a huge foreigner's complex with teachers and exiles from Asia, Africa, Latin America, Eastern and Western Europe. I was able to travel the entire route of the Revolution. Near Chingkangshan, the mountain village where Mao's strategy of peasant organization first took successful root, I saw a poor peasant woman carrying her dead baby boy. He had died from an illness and she cried out in what my Chinese Communist mentor told me was a Buddhist chant to death. I have never forgotten her cry—it was for me one side of the "cry of our times." I wrote a long poem of that title which contrasted peasant life in feudal China with the luxurious life of the Empress. Then the Empress attends a Peking Opera about a daring rebellion of the Monkey King. At the poem's end a verse connects the Chinese Revolution to the Vietnamese—such uprisings against colonial tyranny transformed the "cry of our times" into a chant of resistance.

II. The Night Was Long

The night was long before the liberation
Old China landlord whip foreign warship
Suffering poverty disease exploitation
The night was long before the liberation.

Always popular resistance sometimes war
Taiping Revolution 1851 to 1864
Revolution of 1911 led by Sun Yat-sen
Resistance rising again and again.

These rebellions failed to unify or liberate
Their contribution great but failed to see
That the major obstacles to freedom were three
All had to be removed to reach victory.

Three heavy mountains as the Chinese now say
Foreign imperialism, starting with opium slave trade
Early capitalist production, workers brutalized
Feudalism, landlord-warlord rule of the countryside.

Old Shanghai foreign controlled
Corruption and starvation bought and sold
A few rich Chinese businessmen could profit if they kowtowed
Sign in a Shanghai park said "No Chinese or Dogs Allowed."

Child dead in mine, boss says come back another time
Can you imagine what it must have meant
For the landlord to take away your daughter
When you could not pay an impossibly high rent?

The three heavy mountains had to be removed
Only when that was done
Could liberation be won
So long so long before the rising of the sun.

The night was long before the liberation
Old China landlord whip foreign warship
Suffering poverty disease exploitation
The night was long before the liberation.

To My Class in Peking

From the green of warm September
To the frost of cold December
A tug-of-war, a summer palace walk
Questions, lectures, dialogues, free talks,
This time holds much I will remember.

A foreign-inexpert teacher learned from you
About teaching, and of China, and through
This, of many hands along a strong rope's strands,
Friendship that unites the people of all lands
With the knowledge of what all of us must do.

We sat talking in the room as right outside
The heavy hanging frost lay on the trees,
Heavy, yet spread on every slender branch.
And we could hear too from outside the room
A new building rising, just as I could see
Your progress in the classroom with its sign:
A foreign language is a weapon, a weapon
In the class struggle. The frost lay heavy
And that day I heard a Chinese saying:
When there is frost in the morning,
It will surely be a beautiful day.
It is the same with learning English,
It is the same with the changing world,
Through the heavy frost the sun is rising.

1966

Four Limericks

There was this philosopher Marx
Whose sharp dialectics drew sparks
And up rose the spectre
As he finished the lecture:
Little fish will devour the sharks.

Then up stepped a young lawyer named Lenin
It was fire that he dipped his pen in
When asked why he did it
He replied, "man get with it,
Fight fire with fire," said Lenin.

You've heard much of a student named Mao
Who merely answered the question of how
To win power in China
And what's even finer
Old Mao still remains with us now.

The last one we come to is me
In a class by myself you'll agree
While I rhyme in confusion
People make revolution
Criticizing the hell out of me.

1967

The Curse

The ancient Chinese had a curse—
May you be born
In an important age.

That curse is ours
Our age of civil wars
On Earth
And deep inside our minds.

Men and women torn in two
This torment seems to make
The curse hold true.

But see the fists upraised—
It is no curse to live today
There is horror
But there is also change.

If much of what we see
Marks sure decay
It is our task to build
Upon the ruins today.

We were born in an important age
And that will prove a curse
Only if we fail.

1966

Dover Beach Revisited

The sea is rough tonight
The tide is full, the moon is shattered
Upon the straits;—on the Asian coast the light
Gleams and is gone; the ships of Amerika stand
Forbidding and vast, out in the shaking bay.
Come to the window, the panes are battered
Broken from the long line of spray
For where the sea meets the moon-blanched land,
Listen! You will hear the grating roar
Of bullets which the waves draw back, and fling,
At their return up the high strand,
Begin, and cease, and then again begin,
With staccato cadence quick, and bring
The eternal note of sadness in.

Sophocles long ago
Heard it on the Aegean, and it brought
Into his mind the turbid ebb and flow
Of human misery; we
Find also in the sound a thought
Hearing it by this distant eastern sea.

The Sea of Freedom
Was once too broken, not round earth's shore
Lay like a javelin but still unhurl'd.
But now I surely hear
Its triumphant, long, advancing roar,
Advancing, to the drums
Of the sunlight, over the vast edges drear
And naked shingles of the world.

Ah, love, let us be true
To one another! for the world, which seems
To hold uncertainty and death and pain
Neither joy, nor love, nor light
Now lies before us like a human land of dreams
So various, so beautiful, so new
And we are here as on a vast green plain
Swept by heroic cries of struggle and right
As faraway two armies clash by night.

Note: In this presumptuous spin on the classic Matthew Arnold poem, the strongest emotional elements spring from the original source, not my meagre substitutions. I include it to represent an era as serious as that depicted by Arnold—weaving the "eternal sadness" of the Vietnam war and the "beautiful" and "new" mass movement, exhilarating, filled with love and solidarity. Those of us who supported the Vietnamese people's independence struggle knew their victories were part of the "advancing roar" of the "Sea of Freedom." I read this poem and others at small gatherings of poetry enthusiasts. It was well received, because it was familiar and spoke to our era, but also because Arnold's oceanic cadences lend themselves so beautifully to being spoken aloud. For those gathered then and all "old friends," I freely translate Chairman Mao:

Changsha by Mao Tse-tung

Alone in the autumn cold,
Where the Hsiang River flows north,
I stand at the tip of Orange Island
Looking out at thousands of red hills,
Row after row of crimson forest.
On the turquoise river,
Hundreds of boats contend
Fish glide beneath the clear water.
Eagles strike the sky,
All creatures fight for freedom
Under the frosty firmament.
Alone in the infinity of nature I ask:
Who controls the rise and fall of destiny?

Hundreds of friends used to come here...
Remember the old times?
The years of fullness, when we were students—
Young, brilliant, blooming with powerful arguments,
Boldly casting all restraints aside,
Pointing to our mountains and rivers
Setting people in fiery motion with our words—
To us, rich warlords with a thousand houses
Weren't worth a sack of shit!
Remember still
How, venturing midstream
We struck the water together,
Making waves that stopped
The racing boats?

(and they did indeed make waves...)

Letter to the Draft Board

I.

I sit in jail—an American
My government murders and lies
I am absolutely certain this is so.

I sit in jail—just an American
Today I worked on the prison farm
And not used to the work I am tired.

Only a few hours in the fields
But dead tired—thinking
Of the peasants who work all their lives.

I am tired but cannot sleep
Dead tired—but I cannot sleep
How can any American sleep?

II.

I have talked to some fellow prisoners
And many understand
See past police-imposed facade.

They see their own lives
The young, the old, the black and white
Hard not to see the foot that stomps on you.

But there are some who laugh about death
Some who have returned from Vietnam
Whose eyes are glazed with genocide.

I look at them and cannot sleep
Dead tired—but I cannot sleep
How can any American sleep?

III.

So go to sleep America forget
The ceaseless bombing and the lies
Think positive—life has its rewards.

As you seek to occupy exploit the earth
Just close your eyes and go to sleep
It is so easy to forget.

Yes, America turn off the lights
Lie in electric blankets, rest on soft pillows
Turn on, turn off, and drop out.

Is it easy to sleep, easy to sleep
With ghosts of genocide buried deep
How can any American sleep?

IV.

Dead tired but I cannot sleep, I cry
More for America than for the peasant
For the cry of the peasant is shaking the earth.

My cry is not a cry of sorrow alone
It is not accompanied by tears
It is both a cry and a call to resist.

A call to all to see, not turn away
A call to all new voices of freedom
Saying I am with them.

Dead tired but I cannot sleep
American nightmare before my waking eyes
Awake America my anguished cry—

Awake America, or die.   *1966*

Note: This sincere attempt to practice basic truth telling is a
dramatic and emotional reflection of the times. It was written
at the San Francisco County Jail at San Bruno, where I spent
30 days as the war in Vietnam escalated once again. Anger,
frustration, warning, and a rallying cry are all mixed together
in its bitterness at genocide past and present. Some may
perceive the last line as hyperbole. Perhaps. In this and all
similar cases, I urge all readers to think for themselves!

Sky River

Welcome
Children of the forest
To the place
Where the river
Meets the sky
River meets the sky
Welcome
Children of the forest
To Sky River.

The land belongs to all of us.

Swim naked
In clear waters
Laughing
Dancing in the sun.

Work together
To the rhythm
Love and struggle
There is much that must be done.

The revolution
Is just beginning
Much of the old
Mixes in the new like mud.

Someday we shall see
Women walking free
Enough food for everyone
Already freedom flowers bud.

The rain washes over our land.

Welcome
Children of the forest
To the place
Where the river
Meets the sky
River meets the sky
Welcome
Children of the forest
To Sky River!

Note: While I was more overtly part and partisan of the socio-political and left-wing cultural revolutions, let's not forget those San Francisco roots. True, I started out in the Fillmore district when it was a happening Black community and the Haight-Ashbury when it was an integrated working and middle class neighborhood—hardly known for its non-conformity! Despite world travel in socialist countries where marijuana was verboten, I had plenty of San Fran in my heart, so naturally was strongly affected, as so many of my generation, by what came to be called "youth culture."

I remember very fondly the times my father took me down to North Beach at the height of the Beat upsurge where we sat in "The Bagel Shop" with its open mike and listened to wild poetic improvisations. Then of course I just happened to go to Cornell the same year Timothy Leary (may he unrest in peace) and Richard Alpert (now Ram Dass) had a farm at Millbrook and spread the psychoactive gospel. Various natural psychedelics, such as wood rose seeds, got ground up in Ithaca supermarkets, gulped down with coca-cola, and caused hallucinations way past LSD.

So there was a generous dose of long-haired hippie in me, even though I also I wrote a dialogue between a Hippie and a Red Guard that was published in the National Guardian in which I contrasted, quite unfavorably, a spaced-out non-judgmental hippie with a disciplined, rebellious Red Guard who was dedicated to serving the people. (That was at the start of the Chinese cultural revolution, when it deceptively appeared similar to the mass student movement I was familiar with in the United States.)

Youth culture—birthed by the civil rights and world peace movements, nurtured by blues, jazz, beat and zen, filled with images of ecstatic joy, flowing skirts, bright colors, long hair, beards, overflowing with pacifism and camarade-rie, music and mass gatherings—this rejection of main-stream materialist hypocrisy marked a cultural vitality that put the nail in the coffin of 50s style McCarthyist confor-mity. While Woodstock and Altamont gained fame and infame, there were thousands of other gatherings and celebratory festivals, like the one at Sky River in Oregon. No doubt there were problems and sorrows there too, but I remember a veritable Eden, with thousands of people peacefully assembling, friendly, often nude, sunbathing and diving, gathering near the shore of a river, listening and dancing to music, and feeling that sense of collective solidarity, well-being, sexual relaxation, and youthful freedom that characterized the "culture" at its highest expression.

The Song of Hayakawa or Up Against the Wall Mother Country *(with all due apologies to Henry Wadsworth Longfellow)*

Should you ask me, whence this story
Whence these protests and repressions
With the chantings of the students
With the blow and blood of nightsticks,
With the hard lines of the trusties
With the lying tongues of reagans
With the rushings of great meanings
With their power found in action
And their world reverberations
As of wounds within the monster?
        I should answer, I should tell thee
"From the past and from the present
From the slavery in Southland
From its partner in the Northland
From the fire in the cities
From the poor, the lost, the cursed ones
Where the youth, on plastic campus
Is taught with lies of men in power
I repeat it as I heard it
From the lips of revolution
That musician, that sweet singer."

By the shores of Golden Gateway
By the rotting BART construction
Stood a campus of Glenn Dumke
Son of a dollar Dumke
And behind him rose the trusties
Rose the rantings of the gov'ner
To the tune of corporations.
But the answer that is blowing
In the winds of change that's coming
Also beat the Big Sea Water.
        There the wrinkled old Glenn Dumke
Nursed his puppet Hayakawa
Rocked him in his crooked cradle
Aided by an Alioto
Who provided piggish sinews
Tried to still his sweat by saying
"Yes the arm of force will save thee."
But no lullaby the chanting
"On strike, let's shut it down!"
Who are these who fill the campus
With their fists upraised in Anger
"On strike, let's shut it down!"

Many things his masters taught him
After Summerskill had fallen
Down the hole to Ethiopia
After Smith of lacking lustre
Found the burden too disturbing.
Many things his masters taught him
Of the ways to handle protests
Of the ways to dodge the issues
And protect the status quo.
Trained him in the hard line holler
Showed him blood they called the system
That has tried to rule the world.
Showed policemen beating warriors
In the Death Dance of their Order...
And the sight made him excited
As a ride on roller coaster
In the time of his tenth birthday
With strong stomach he enjoyed it.
On the tubes of their mass media
Taught him how to be flamboyant
How to represent the racism
That had placed his own strong people
In war camps in California.
        And they pumped him full of letters,
Words, syllables, call it hot air...
But they called the stuff semantics.
Told him problems all were verbal
Bluster all that now was needed.

        But the lips of revolution
Answered back, "no Hayakawa."
Answered back with strength of numbers
Echoed past the armored legions
With their pistols drawn and pointed.
Answered back to Hayakawa
Said the issues must be answered
Education must have meaning
Help to change the present order.
For our people whom you've stepped on
Now are waking, now must study
Lessons taught by your oppression
Learn the history you've stolen.
That is why we on this campus
Demand self-determination.

Answered back, "no Hayakawa."
And their rising calls were answered
By some elders of their peoples
Saying, "we will stand between you.
When the swine approach your marches,
We'll not let a generation
Lose its youth and lose its struggle
For your struggle is our struggle
You are sisters, you are brothers."

Forth upon the Golden Gateway
By the rotting BART construction
With the purse strings of his masters
Fastened to his head and shoulders
Hayakawa launched new efforts
To subdue the rising rebels
After watching from his window
All those beaten and arrested
He talked with an Alioto
And announced a "new" position
To preserve his falling campus
To divide the chanting students
But the pigs still root on campus
And the students hold more rallies
As the struggle is continued
From a new and higher level.

Maybe ups and downs of struggle
And new twistings of the trusties
May discourage and new methods
Will be needed, still the song of
Hayakawa and the dirges of his masters
Can have only one conclusion,
As the struggle always deepens
As the people see deceptions
And increase their ways of protest
As they organize their numbers.

Then the song of Hayakawa
Who seems strong but whose repressions
Only mean that he is failing
Then the song of Hayakawa
Ends, "Farewell O Hayakawa."
As students black-brown-white in color
Crush his fiery puppet pratings
And the winds announce their message
Sing— "Farewell O Hayakawa."
Thus departed Hayakawa
Hayakawa's strings left dangling
And the masters behind curtains
Sought in this their time of sunset
Still to still the rising protest.

But their time's not long in coming
And their sunset is our sunrise
Sunrise too in other nations
Where they send their thieving armies
Many nations like the campus
And whose people are as students
Seeking self-determination.

Talk about an education
We have gained one in these hours
And the song of Hayakawa
Every note a lesson learned.

December 1968

Note: This poem was written during the first of a series of
student rebellions at San Francisco State, as campuses across
the country exploded with student demands for freedom of
speech, equality, relevance, and self-determination. It was
first recited on a late-night KPFA show humorously entitled
"Surplus Prophets." While this poem, as published in *The
Movement* newspaper, did include the phrase, "with all due
apologies to Henry Wadsworth Longfellow," we should also
add that Longfellow, despite great poetic talent and prover-
bial good intentions—and understanding that people are
creatures of their times— also might have some apologies to
make —to the Native peoples themselves!

Heavier Than Mount Tai   for Fred Hampton

I.

You jive ass fools
Who practice genocide
Shall surely die
Us brothers and sisters
Shall survive
And dig it
No matter who you kill
The revolution stays alive.

Power to the People!

Wherever death
May down us

It'll be welcome
So long as this

Power to the People!

Our battle cry
Is picked up on
That another hand
Take up our weapons

Power to the People!

That sisters and brothers
Step on up to sing
Our funeral spirituals
With the rat tat tat of

Power to the People!

Machine guns
And new cries
Of battle
And of victory.

Power to the People!

You jive ass fools
Shall die
We shall survive
No matter who you kill
The revolution stays alive.

II.

The streets are screaming and the lights are out
The streets are screaming and the lights are out
People got so much to do, so much to figure out.

The times are heavy and indigo the mood
The times are heavy and indigo the mood
When they took him they took a heavy dude.

They shot him in his sleep, wife at his side
They shot him in his sleep, Deborah at his side
She carries a new revolutionary deep inside.

He was dreaming of how power conquers sorrow
He dreamt about how power could stomp sorrow
His head and body getting ready for tomorrow.

The streets are screaming and the lights are out
The streets are screaming and the lights are out
We got so much to do, so much to work on out.

The slavemasters shall die and we shall survive
The slavemasters shall die and we shall survive
No matter who they kill, the revolution stays alive.

III.

Hey, this man could talk
Could really run it down
That's cause he'd been there
Talk about payin' dues
He'd cut through from the blues
To rapping melodies
That wailed on freedom.

Get into it, he said:
"We're sayin' that theory's cool,
But theory with no practice
Ain't worth shit
You got to have them both."
"We have a theory about feedin' kids free
What'd we do? Put it into practice—
That's how people learn.
A lot of people don't know how serious it is,
Maybe think the children we feed ain't hungry.
Well, I don't know no five-year-olds
That can't act well, but I do know that
If they not hungry we sure got some actors—
We got some five-year-olds could take
The mother fuckin' academy award!"

"Last week they had a whole week
Dedicated to the hungry in Chicago,
Talkin' about the starvation rate
Went up fifteen percent—
Over here, where everyone could eat.
Why? Because of capitalism."

"Stay into it," he said:
"Just as fast
As the people can go,
That's just as fast
As we can take it."

"We must be sure we ain't missin'
The people in the valley.
In the valley we know that we
Can learn to understand the life of the people."

"What with all the bullshit out there
You can come to consider yourself
Up on the mountain top.
I may have even sometimes considered myself
Up on the mountain top…"

"Going into the valley is a dangerous thing,
You got to be serious, you got to be ready…
I am so revolutionary proletarian intoxicated
That I cannot be gastronomically intimidated."

Hey, that man was 21 years old, could talk,
Could organize, and fight, and run it down,
Talk about payin' dues
He'd cut through from the blues
To rapping melodies
That wailed on freedom.

We shall survive
No matter who they kill
The revolution
Stays alive.

IV.
In Chicago
The people come
To see the place
Where a leader
Was murdered
The people come
To pass the coffin
Crying
With their fists raised high.

Come the mothers
Souls scarred
Who've had to scrub
The white man's floors
Raised their children
Hoping for the sun
While being spit upon.
They knew him
And he knew them.

Come street brothers
Who stand around the liquor stores
Who fill the air
With the laughter of oppression
Who sometimes sigh
And sing a down-home blues
Hoping for the sun
While being spit upon
They knew him
And he knew them.

Come the young and old
The nurses and the mailmen
Workers, welfare, unemployed
The rebels and resisters
The children come
The whites who have begun to act—
All hoping for the sun
They knew him

And he knew them
Our work has just begun.

V.

How can there be a murder, and yet a life?
How can there be a blues, without no strife?
How can there be a valley, without no heights?
How can there be a revolution, with all their might?

A murder when avenged, it brings forth life
A blues, when it is sung, can conquer strife
A valley, when it rises, there are no heights
A revolution, when it's needed, it stays alive.

Fred Hampton, Chairman, Illinois Black Panther Party

Another Day

Two men fight hand to hand
In the light of early dawn
As around them
An occupying army
Is defeated.

A man runs down the street
In the black of ghetto night
And is murdered by a cop
As around them
Businesses burst in avenging flames.

A child cries of hunger
In the black and white
Of day and night
His parents broken
While a few can eat their fill.

A woman and a man make love
But afterward
Must ask themselves what they can do
To make this world
Fit for their children.

Also
Today
They shot
A rocket
To the moon.

Seeds of Revolution   for Jeff Sharlet, editor of *Vietnam GI*, who died of cancer in 1969, at the age of 27.

Brothers and Sisters
Part of us is dead.
Let it be forever known
That he served the people.

Let it be understood
That he did time in Vietnam
That he knew and loved the men
Who write the letters home:

"What kind of world is this
To kill on a command
What right do I have to do that?
What am I doing over here?
Mama, I am so mixed up, help me
I don't know which way to turn
What to believe in or not to believe in
I am lost in this big lonely world
Mama, give me something to believe in."

He knew and loved the men
Who write the letters home
And when he came home
He gave them something to believe in.

Themselves, together, to believe in.
Not long ago he said:
"We felt a newspaper
Was the best way to begin...

To talk to the enlisted men
The guys on the bottom
Help bridge the gap between
The movement and the people."

He was a quiet, vital guy
Who thought before he spoke,
Looked straight in peoples' eyes
And those who listened learned.

So fucking many times
People doing the hardest work
Are taken for granted
Because they talk less and do more.

Modesty building the movement
For conceit turns it around
He listened to what people said
And remembered what he heard.

He travelled many miles
Into the valley of the people
Always learning
Planting seeds of revolution.

Talking to the men in uniform
Feeling the pulse of the people
Working long hours to help
The paper serve their needs.

He told us
That people in the movement
Have to overcome their backgrounds
To take a step into America.

Told us that to plant the seeds
People had to change
Change through their experience
He spoke the truth.

He was aware
Of all the splits and arguments
Of which groups moved which ways
Aware of ideology.

But he always judged
On practice, knowing that
Some internal contradictions
Grow out of isolation.

For more than anything
He worked for the people at the bottom
And his gauge for judgment
Was the wisdom of the people.

A good man.
So many things
Embodied in those three words
Death leaves so much unsaid.

Sadness and fury
As death goes down around us.
The staccato of their clubs and guns
Sisters and Brothers burned and shot and hung.
Minds eaten up
Fear twisted to insanity.
The testing of the bombs,
The pesticides
The dust inside the mines:
Congealed in cancerous disease.
Sadness and fury
As death goes down around us.

Brothers and Sisters
He is fighting with us
The rapping and the writing
The seeds have taken root...

Courage from his courage
Example of his deeds,
For Jeff is dead...
Like Johnny Appleseed.   July 1969

Note: One of the most important sections of the anti-war move-
ment was made up of antiwar GIs and their supporters. *The
Movement* newspaper, where this poem was first published,
carried articles on organizing in the military, with a regular
column called "Shaking the Big Stick." My sister Miranda, now
an internationally-known muralist and cultural activist, helped
run an antiwar GI coffeehouse, the Shelter Half, near Fort Lewis
in Washington state. Within this movement, Jeff Sharlet was an
authentic leader, modest and sincere, calm, a good listener, with
iron determination and large vision. His death was a tragedy for
all who knew him and the cause we embraced. I was deeply
honored when the family wrote to say they had engraved my
words on his gravestone: "Courage from his courage..."

To The Oakland Seven from the Oakland 10,000

I.

When I went for my physical
At the Oakland Induction Center
They were doing some construction
So us poor victims had to enter
Through a side door to the pounding of jackhammers
Like the pounding in our heads.

But at the sound of sidewalk cracking
Which sorta shook us up at first
(We didn't flash on what it was)
The crash had hardly passed when
One cat turned to me, and flipped a V, and said
Hope it's those demonstrators at it again,

Like, during, what'd they call it?
Stop the Draft Week, a year ago,
Yeh, that was it. They raised all kinds of hell.

Yeh, I was down here then.
Hey, man, so was I. I came down and ran around,
Even though I missed work.
Hell No We Won't Go, we said.

And look at us now...where do you work?

Down at that auto plant in Fremont.

I told him that I knew the seven dudes
They busted for conspiracy
And when he asked what kind of guys they were
I told him they were all good cats...
They had problems just like you or me
But they had a lotta guts,
And wives, and lovers, and plenty of friends.
Told him they were into different things
But they'd been picked out, were on the line,
And that I didn't know what would happen to them.
We both agreed they should be free.

68

Hey man...you see the doctor yet?

Uh Uh. How you tryin' to get out?

Aw man...dig this lineup for the slaughterhouse.
Sure hope it's those demonstrators at it again.

II.

That was a while ago
And tonight the Oakland Seven were acquitted.
Innocent of conspiracy
Guilty of raising an issue
That the jury could well understand:
With a son in Nam
Dollars down the drain
Defeat upon defeat
Deception on deception
Caught napalm-handed
A grandson going to be drafted
Ghettoes going up in flames
A genocidal shame
A brother dead.
Tonight the Oakland Seven were acquitted.

A victory to treasure
In an as yet too small collection
And Charlie Garry knows his stuff
Nobody says the courts are just
Just that there's nothin' like a line
Whose time has come
And that constant education
Can cut through obfuscation,
And that we still got some rights if we fight.
Tonight the Oakland Seven were acquitted.

A victory
But still a long long ways to go.
Where will the 7 go?
Where will we 10,000 go?

Maybe in different directions
Maybe head toward the same place
In different ways
But one thing remains
Once the 7 were here together
With us 10,000
And they were right
And we won
a victory.

New cases coming up
New battles
We'll remember this then.

New battles
But raise your fist
In happiness tonight
For the Oakland Seven.

And hope it's those demonstrators at it again.

Note: Here's to each one of the Oakland 7 and also and most
especially to Karen Koonan, who, if the indictment for
conspiracy had accurately represented the leadership, would
have been much more than a co-conspirator, as she played a
central role in this militant demonstration. Here's to all of
the 10,000, to Charlie Garry and the phalanx of other attor-
neys who played prominent and sometimes daring and
dangerous roles in the many movements of that time. Here's
to *The Movement* newspaper, its editorial board, some of
whom wound up indicted for conspiracy for Stop-the-Draft
Week, to its editors-in-chief Terry Cannon, Joseph Blum, and
Arlene Eisen. I remember me and Joe winding through the
streets and navigating the barricades during those demon-
strations and many others. *The Movement* headlined the
event "From Protest to Resistance," and, however one saw
the significance of that demonstration, there was no question
that during those times a line was crossed by many activists.
The level of government violence against Vietnam, the level
of repression against the civil rights and Black liberation
movements, along with the revolutionary mood around the
world and here at home all caused many to envision the
possibility of revolutionary change, to condemn the compro-
mises with injustice represented by efforts to reform the
system, and, to put one's body on the line to stop the war.

In Memory of Al Lannon

He was a sailor
Got organized
During the Russian Revolution
Went to the Lenin school in Moscow
Came back
Became an organizer.

Once when he was a delegate
To an early national convention
Of the CPUSA he came to New York
To discover that the convention committee
For security reasons
Had arranged for some to stay in the suburbs
In the homes of "fellow travellers"
Instead of the usual
Crowded Manhattan tenements.

He went to the address assigned him
Knocked on the door
A maid answered and he was ushered in
Told to wait in the library
That the host would be with him shortly.

As he waited
He marvelled at all the books.
The host arrived
The organizer asked
If he'd read all the books
The host replied that he'd read most of them.
The organizer said he was amazed
There were so many books
Said he had read so little.
Well, said the host, after all
When the workers seize power
They'll need intellectual guidance.

The organizer looked him in the eye
Then took his bags from off the floor
Inside his head he heard a line from the Internationale
He turned and spoke, before he slammed the door,
"Mister, don't do us any favors—
We want no condescending saviors."

Note: Al Lannon was a legendary Communist, national leader,
maritime unionist, and one of my father's closest comrades and
confidantes, even when they disagreed. I got a chance to spend
some hours talking with Al and my father, and during one of
those conversations Al told me the story in the poem.

In Contempt

When the chairman is in chains
Denied his rights
He stands and speaks
Defiant man among defiant men.

In the beginning
It was just Huey and me
Then there was little Bobby.
Now we have a party
The chapters spread
Across the country.

When the chairman is in chains
In Nazi courts
He stands and speaks
Defiant man among defiant men.

There is no justice
For black people, no liberty
I demand
The right of self defense
No fascist pig
Can take away my dignity.

When the chairman is in chains
Bound in contempt
He stands and speaks
Defiant man among defiant men.

We had to speak
When we began to see
Liberation in the colony
The roots of revolution
In the mother country
When we defined the enemy.

When the chairman is in chains
And framed
He stands and speaks
Defiant man among defiant men.

We understood when we began
Now you can understand
You're either part of the problem
Or part of the solution.
They can jail a revolutionary
But not the revolution.

Where were you
When they chained him to a chair?
Where were you
When they denied him air?

He cannot be gagged
Because his voice is ours.

The chairman is in chains
All of us make the attempt
Till he is free and we have won
All of us stand in contempt.

Note: At the conspiracy trial following the 1968 Chicago
demonstrations during the Democratic Party convention,
Bobby Seale, then Chairman of the Black Panther Party, was
found in contempt of court for seeking to defend himself. In
contemptible racist style he was bound and gagged in the
courtroom. The last line, "All of us stand in contempt"
echoes the song "In Contempt," one of the most militant
songs to emerge from the relatively small but extremely
courageous resistance against McCarthyism. Lines from the
song include: "Build high, build wide your prison walls, let
there be room enough for all, who hold you in contempt—
build wide, that all the land be locked inside..." Later, "The
poets dreaming still of peace, the playful children, the wild
geese..." Then, "When you have jailed both moon and sun,
and chained the poems one by one, and trapped each trouble
making breeze, then you can throw away your keys..." One
verse proclaims: "The birds who still insist on song, the
sunlit streams still running strong, the flowers still blazing
red and blue—like fists are in contempt of you!"

A Way of Speaking

Speak secretly
Because the walls have ears.
Secretly, as in love
And revolution.

Actions test of truth
And bravery in act
Not in reckless words
Shouted on tapped telephones.

A revolutionary takes chances
When chances must be taken
A chance at any other time
Is perhaps to waste a life,

Perhaps many lives.
And a revolutionary
Treasures life so much
He, or she, is willing to give it.

Does it aid your ego
To boast of plans already made
Or give away a confidence
Or speak of who you saw with who?

Remember,
As you speak
That you may be endangering
The one you tell.

"There will be
No more pain
If you tell us
The names."

Always speak
What is necessary for success
Too much, too often, too soon
Guarantees failure.

These are the times
When the fist of fascism closes
But we also have our fists
And the work hardened muscle of history.

The peoples of the earth
Are with us
So our cautions
Do not come from fear.

In spite of our mistakes
Divisions and despairs
We have not acquiesced
We have begun to learn resistance.

Do not be afraid to act.
Act with the energy of an occupied nation.
The energy of knowing you have
One more day outside the concentration camps.

Expansion yields protection
Explain, persuade, and organize
Do not be afraid to learn
Ways to speak to the needs of the people.

Note: This poem was also published in *The Movement* newspaper, with a photograph of a group of Vietnamese freedom fighters smiling and singing around a campfire.

Song of a Thread   by Ho Chi Minh

My mother is a blossom,
My body is soft,
I am cotton.

Once I was so weak
I could be torn to pieces,
Whenever I was touched
Even by gentle breezes.

When I became thread,
I was still not strong,
I could not do anything by myself.

Who says a single thread is strong?
The longer I am,
The weaker I am,
Who pays any attention to a single small thread?

But, there are many millions like me,
We come together in criss-crossing patterns
We weave together into beautiful cloth,
Stronger than silk and more lasting than leather,
Who would dare tear us apart now?

That's real force,
That's true glory.

All people unite!
To be free we must fight!
Working hand in hand we weave
Tapestries of victory!

Note: Original translation by the author, with the assistance
of the Union of Vietnamese students in the United States.
They were a wonderful group of college-age students who
held many educational events in the Bay Area. An older
Vietnamese man, Van Luy, a truly dedicated patriot (and
great chef), provided counsel and encouragement, and was
a revolutionary example of wisdom and modesty to us all.

State of Emergency
(recited to a large rally at San Francisco's Union Square)

Sisters and Brothers Everywhere
It is time for us to declare
A state of emergency
Worldwide and Inside.

This does not mean suicide
Or frantic desperation
But rising to the situation
Total mobilization
Does not mean
Errors purely military
But does mean
Doing what is necessary

Doing everything we can
In every way possible
For these are times which try our souls
Times which cry out cry out cry out
For acts of effective and sustained resistance.

Resistance aimed well to aid
Our sisters and brothers winning in Vietnam
To impede and disable the war machine
Combining truth, justice, love for humanity
To reach and serve as many people as we can
In this situation
Energy and determination
Finding deep within ourselves
The courage and the care
All that we can give
To defend the right to live...to live....to live.

In Black or Brown communities or on campuses
When they declare states of emergency
It means curfews, restrictions on the sale of gasoline
Mass arrests, National Guardsmen, police
Beatings and murders increase increase increase.

So-called Governors and Presidents
Declare these states
But today all of us are so empowered
Feel the deep responsibility
When we declare an extreme emergency.

Our declaration not like theirs—no way
For ours goes to the meaning of the phrase:

Emergency!

Something is emerging
Emerging very rapidly
A situation crying out
To the heroism in each one of us
Demands preparation for contingencies
Learn first aid for minds and bodies
Emergency
Reach teach always reaching out
Acts of resistance defiant shout
Chant freedom sound to bring the monster down
That is what it has to be about.

Preparing for the worst the worst the worst
While nurturing the best
Giving warmakers no rest no rest no rest

Something is emerging
A spirit is surging
Victory victory victory to Vietnam

As suddenly
In acts of increasing atrocity
The entire Earth
Has been thrown into
A state of emergency

Victory to Vietnam!
Support the Seven Points!
Blockade the Bay!
Dienbienphu in '72!

78

There are many ways to fight
Many things to do which are right.

Now, something that is hard to say
Because of what it implies for our lives
Though our lives are threatened anyway
Hard to say
Because it may mean our lives
But it must be said today
The time has arrived...

If not now, when?

The time arrives
If life is to survive and grow
Blood will flow
Struggle is so hard, takes time
That much we have begun to know
And though the words are heavy to say
Heavier still to do
Still their aim is absolutely true:

So say it loud
And say it clear
For everyone to hear
From the mountains
To the prairies
To the oceans
White with foam...

BRING THE WAR HOME!

Memorial to Nguyen Thai Binh

Red
Blue
Yellow
Candle
Flame

My name
Is Thai Binh
In Vietnamese
Thai Binh
Means Peace

My parents
Gave me that name
To express
The deepest aspiration
Of our heroic nation

People of the World
My name
Is Thai Binh
Though I may die
We shall win

People of the World
Take aim
Raise the flag of liberation
Red blue yellow
Candle flame

Note: Nguyen Thai Binh was a Vietnamese student who came to study in the United States. Active in protests for democracy and independence, he allegedly attempted to hijack an airliner to call attention to his people's cause. When shot and killed by security guards, the " bomb" turned out to be an orange. This poem was read at one of many memorials for him. He was known as a sincere and committed idealist with a gentle personality and love of children. Thai Binh means "peace won through struggle" and it became the middle name of Anna, my older daughter. The eternal candle also burns for the Buddhist monks of Vietnam who immolated themselves in protest of the war, as did Quaker Norman Morrison on the steps of the Pentagon, Alice Herz in Detroit, and Roger Laporte at the United Nations. The fabric of resistance, interwoven with countless individual and collective acts of courage, shines with the ultimate sacrifice of these dedicated souls.

On to Victory   for Ho Chi Minh

I. We Say

He lived to hear
His nieces and his nephews
Sing the songs of revolution
And they sing.

He lived to see
The towers of the new
Rising ever higher
And they build.

He lived to touch
The outstretched hand of freedom
To hold it in his hand
And they grasp it.

He lived to smell
The flowers of the children
In the air of independence
And they breathe.

He lived to taste
The fruits of victory
To sip the tea of happiness
We must win.

II. He Said

I remember when
I became a man
Despising oppression
Determined to end it.

I remember when
I travelled and studied
Through practice becoming
A Communist.

And I remember when
Imprisoned and tortured
The poetry of hope
Broke through the bars.
It was not me, it was the people
We organized and fought
So many fell
But fell in victory.

And even now
The struggle deepens
Fighting while we build
To freedom.

III. We Say

Uncle, comrade, teacher
Pushed up from
Oppression's soil
To march among us.

Uncle, comrade, teacher
We learn from you
To gather millions
Who will guard your memory.

Uncle, comrade, teacher
You march among us
Leader of the revolution
Bringing power to the people.

Grief at first
But it is overcome
By all that you have done
By all that we must do.

High on every terraced mountain
Rises rice of revolution
Join us in the harvest
We shall win.

September 1969

Note: Tom Mosher, a government agent, in his testimony to the Senate Internal Security Committee, actually called my poem to Ho Chi Minh "an Onward Christian Soldiers for the radical movement." I was pleased that the entire poem, as it appeared in *The Movement* newspaper with a nice photograph of Uncle Ho screened behind it, was thereby entered into the historical record for posterity. While I have nothing but contempt for Mosher, who I knew slightly when he was associated with the outstanding community organization named Jobs Or Income Now (JOIN) and related radical community organizing efforts in Chicago, and who also attended Stanford University, in an ironic way this was one of my better reviews! I have no wish to elevate Ho or anyone else to radical sainthood, but I believe him to be one of the greatest individuals of the 20th century, a brilliant and dedicated organizer, and a superb if occasional poet.

Sonnet for the Fall   (1972, 1998, 2002)

To you who feel these lines in summer's sun
The seasons change as child begins to crawl
It is the monsoon time in Vietnam
It is just days—just days—before the fall.
Leaves of our lives turn crimson turn turn turn
For there is always more for us to learn
Seeds of the spring to harvest in the fall
And all signs say this spring will take our all.
It's time to gather all we've grown we must
Unite to find the best in each of us
In sacrifice to autumn's freedom call
It is just days—just days— before the fall.

For victory of Vietnam world sings
For all the joy that liberation brings.

The Perfume River   for My Loc

The Perfume River gently winds
Through city of historic lore
You told me how you loved to watch
The sunset from its shore.

The Perfume River gently winds
Through city that has seen
So many years, so many tears,
And so much suffering.

The Perfume River gently winds
Yet has invincible persistence
The water wears away the stone
And Hue has always meant resistance.

In the book you lent to me
I read of Dinh Phu Nhan
In the resistance underground
She served as liaison.

Savage tortures after her arrest
In first years of this century
But the will to live in freedom
Triumphed over cruelty.

Asking for a night's respite
Said she'd make a full confession
Instead she wrote indictment
Of colonial oppression.

She wrote her last three poems in blood
Biting her fingers until they bled
Wrote on the walls of her prison cell
They murdered her. She is not dead.

Comrade Dinh Phu Nhan lives on
In united heart of Vietnam
Just as she carried messages
From Hue up to Haiphong.

As Perfume River gently winds
Your eyes looked back in memory
Images of schoolgirls all in white
To childhood and your family.

I asked about temples and tombs
Beautiful, you said, in their way,
But also served as reminders
Of exploitation that held sway.

You described one whose ornate detail
Aped French colonialist style
You spoke movingly of the workers
Hauling huge stones by hand for miles.

Their labor and their sweat live on
In working unity of today
Not in the palaces and tombs
In struggles of the poor of Hue.

For Perfume River gently winds
Yet has invincible persistence
The water wears away the stone
And Hue has always meant resistance.

In '68 the battle reached new heights
Despite horrible U.S. attack
Hue's clarion counter-offensive
Helped break the invader's back.

And today
How beautiful must be
The sunset on the Perfume River
That marks the dawn of victory.

Ancient capital
As river winds into the sea
A flag now lights your citadel
The flag of the PRG.

And you My Loc, daughter of Hue
Knowing in ways I've never known
The terror and agony of war
How often you must think of home.

The Perfume River gently winds
Through city of historic lore
You told me how you loved to watch
The sunset from its shore.

They Are Bombing the Dikes

THEY ARE BOMBING THE DIKES

THEY ARE BOMBING THE DIKES

THEY MAY DENY IT BUT

THEY ARE BOMBING THE DIKES

Fifteen million people
Live in the delta
Destruction of the dikes
Could mean that many die
Fields destroyed
Cutting off food supply
Bombing of dikes
Classified as one of the worst war crimes—
For destroying Dutch dikes
A Nazi commander in World War II
Was executed.

THEY ARE BOMBING THE DIKES

THEY MAY SAY IT ISN'T SO BUT WE KNOW

BECAUSE THE VIETNAMESE SAY SO

MANY REPORTERS HAVE SEEN IT

THE DIKES ARE BEING BOMBED

SYSTEMATICALLY

That children's story
About the little boy who put his finger in
To stop the flood
Until help arrived thus saving many lives...

The entire people of Vietnam
Preparing for every eventuality

We
Could have a lot to do
To help prevent the nightmare
From coming true

Season of monsoon
July to September

REMEMBER WHEN NIXON
WENT TO EXPRESS HIS SORROW
FOR THE VICTIMS OF HEAVY FLOODS?

THEY ARE BOMBING THE DIKES
NOT ONLY THAT
NOT ONLY THAT
THEY ARE ALSO SEEDING THE CLOUDS

THEY ARE BOMBING THE DIKES
THEY ARE SEEDING THE CLOUDS

SEEDING THE CLOUDS
TO TRY AND CAUSE MORE RAIN AND FLOOD
SEEDING THE CLOUDS

WITH BLOOD.

Note: The above poem was published in the *Liberated Guardian,* a national newspaper of the time based in New York City.

Prose Poem: Peace Agreement

The day the headlines screamed peace agreement I
watched two plainclothes police beat a Black youth
bloody as they busted him. The youth struggled and
fought. After they shoved him in the car they laughed
a bit at the battle—checked out the blood on the fender
of the car where they'd pinned him. Just as they were
leaving one shouted, "Damn, I lost my wristwatch,"
then he said, "oh, no, here it is, it's over there," and as
he walked over he told the gathered crowd, "It's a
Mickey Mouse wristwatch." And so it was. As he bent
to pick it up the young Black man standing next to me
spit twice on the ground, saying under his breath,
"dirty motherfuckers." An elderly Black man standing
next to him said to a few of the group, "It'll be a half-
hour before they get him to the station. They ain't
finished with him." He kept repeating variations of the
same thing for the next few minutes, shaking his head,
shaking his head, and that was the day the headlines
screamed peace agreement.

**Tet 1977
Rhetorical Question**

Lunar New Year
Moon begins another revolution
Cancer of sectarianism
Takes its fatal toll
Why can't we gather together
Toward common goal?

Without the moon and gravity
Would there be tides upon the sea?
Without a working unity
Can there be chance for victory?

Anti-War Rally Golden Gate Park

She stood in the falling rain
She spoke:
My Loc, Vietnamese woman
Studying in the disunited States
A beautiful clear light around her as
She stood in the falling rain, explained
The seven-point peace proposal
Put forward by the
Provisional Revolutionary Government
She stood in the falling rain
Spoke in a calm and vibrant tone
Said, "In Vietnam we have a saying:
Gentle water wears away the hardest stone."

This Country They Call Free *(partly to the tune of...)*

This country they call free
Land of hypocrisy
To thee we sing
Land where the Indians died
In racist genocide
Where slavery was pilgrim's pride
Can freedom ring?

Our past is filled with pain
Bullets of profit rain
Down hard upon the millions slain
For them we sing

We know what must be done
Despite their planes and guns
Our fight for freedom can be won
Our hearts take wing

And fly above their might
As sunrise out of night
We fight for what we know is right
And freedom bring

Not for ourselves alone
Are seeds of freedom sown
The crops we harvest now have grown
Into a world wide thing

As those in other lands
Take power in their hands
At home we raise the same demands
Let freedom ring

Ring out across the seas
In chants of victories
For you as for Vietnamese
Let freedom ring...

This country they call free
Land of hypocrisy
To thee we sing
Land where the Indians died
In racist genocide
Where slavery was pilgrim's pride
Can freedom ring?

For Wounded Knee and Liberty

Strangers from some distant shore
Invade our land, resistance war
They raped and pillaged all our lands
Tore treaties up with bloody hands
In river sand of Wounded Knee
Killed women, children, elderly
Outlawed our dances and our nations
Locked us up on reservations
But we will rise again you see
For Wounded Knee and Liberty.

Chorus:

Rejoice O Native Land Rejoice
To tyrants never bend the knee
But join with heart and soul and voice
For Wounded Knee and Liberty.

(The chorus is adapted from and can be sung to the tune of the old U.S. revolutionary anthem, "For Jefferson and Liberty.")

Attica (as broadcast)

"What has happened here is but the sound before the fury of those who are oppressed. " (L.D. Barkley, one of the leaders killed at Attica)

Attica
The name is burned
Red hot upon our brains
Pain rains down
Attica
The name is burned
Red hot upon our brains
Burned
War without terms.

Tonight, the autumn leaves
Blood red are shed
Like tears in Attica
Wind of rebellion cries out
Through the branches
Of the tree of liberty
Oh say can you see
By the dawn's early light:
We have to fight.

> Like a leaf clings to a tree
> People cling to liberty.

Wind of rebellion
Cries out through the branches
Voices of prisoners
Whirling in the hurricane of history
We are men, we are not beasts
And we do not intend to be beaten and driven as such
Dogs are treated better than we

Cries out the deepest truth
For us to see
"To oppressed people all over the world
We got the solution
The solution is unity..."
Attica
Unmistakable sign—the fire this time.

And still we sing

Revolutionary soul
Takes wing
Flies carefully
From cell to cell
From mouth to mouth
From house to house
You, listening there—Prepare.

Sisters and Brothers
Our name is Attica.

Attica
The name is burned
Red hot upon our brains
Pain rains down
Attica
The name is burned
Red hot upon our brains
Burned
War without terms.

Tonight, the autumn leaves
Blood red are shed
Like tears in Attica
Wind of rebellion cries out
Through the branches
Of the tree of liberty
Oh say can you see
By the dawn's early light:
We have to fight.

Note: The phrase "war without terms," is from prison revolution-
ary George Jackson. The historical significance of the Attica
Rebellion has not been accurately assessed. Only when this society
and world realize the tortuously inhumane and non-correctional
nature of current systems of punishment will the Attica clarion
call, uniting across races, sound in its full glory. Among those who
"here gave their lives" was Sam Melville, a white revolutionary
convicted of bombings against corporate targets in New York.
Another poem of mine on Attica said: "Sam would have wanted
us to say, when he went down, he went the way of old John
Brown." Along with the eloquent courage of George and Jonathan
Jackson, Ruchell Magee, the San Quentin 6, all the Attica brothers,
and many others, these rebellions will be seen as precursor to a
worldwide transformation toward re-education and respect for
human rights—an end to the barbarism and torture practiced
routinely by many regimes. For more on these struggles, the
Freedom Archives (www.freedomarchives.org) has a CD on San
Quentin and Attica entitled *Prisons on Fire.* Attica, the name is
burned, red hot upon our brains...

Epitaph for J. Edgar Hoover (1972)

May worms investigate
Each flabby fold of flesh
May maggots tap each nerve
Bugs bug every cell
May all the creeping agents
Of bacteria and decay
Have a field day
Eating out your eyes
Which once were peepholes
May infiltrating cancers of the blood
Clog your heart
As final hearings start
To determine the causes
Of the subversion
Of your own body.

For you, no rest in peace
May your unrest never cease

When dead
You can no longer see
Communists beneath your bed
And as you lie inside the earth
Much as you would like to stop them
Much as their beauty you despise
Bright red flowers shall surely rise.

The day you died
Great Indochinese victories
A fitting world situation
For your disintegration.

May worms investigate
Each flabby fold of flesh
May maggots tap each nerve
Bugs bug every cell
And may you forever rot
In special hell
For fascists and torturers of world history
Who have only one redeeming quality:
Their total evil helped people to see
Why we must fight to be free.

Note: The previous poem synthesizes my lifelong fierce hatred for J. Edgar Hoover and total defiance of what he symbolized. The hatred is rooted in the anti-Communist and unconstitutional repression experienced from my earliest childhood, with the FBI knocking on the door, phones tapped, fear spread, jobs lost, investigations, imprisonments, the execution of the Rosenbergs, the Korean War. This hatred of Hoover was strengthened first by my awareness of and then my participation in resistance to this repression. The acts of resistance I saw were many, large and small: Refusing to give away left-wing book collections, going underground in some cases, speaking out—against the Korean war, for an end to the cold war, against nuclear war and bomb testing, picketing to integrate ballrooms, agitating inside the Armed Forces for racial equality, marching on strike lines, going to see the great banned film *Salt of the Earth*, listening and going to concerts of Paul Robeson, the Almanac Singers, Pete Seeger and Malvina Reynolds, defying gangs of violent right-wing vigilantes attacking Paul Robeson and thousands of progressive picnic gatherers in Peekskill New York, hiding a leaflet-making mimeograph machine in a fake dresser in your basement, standing up on Constitutional grounds to the various House and Senate committees and resisting other witchhunt inquisitions and so-called loyalty oaths.

This courageous resistance took many forms and it was quite an amazing and transforming experience to have been born into it. Each new trauma nourished my enmity for Hoover and the FBI. This hatred was deepened by the vicious lies bred by the anti-Communist hysteria, with rabid racism at its core, culminating in Hoover's vile death list of African-American leaders, as part of his murderous and unconstitutional Cointelpro spy and infiltration program. Hoover was also a key player in the earlier, 1919/1920 Palmer Raids against radicals, socialists, and the foreign born. I really hated this man. I rarely say this about anyone—I hated his GUTS! The poem is a synthesis of that hatred, mixed maliciously in with my childhood remembrance of that ghoulish and graphic Halloween-type rhyme about death... "the worms crawl in, the worms crawl out..." and another one about "great green gobs of gopher guts." The later revelations about J. Edgar's corruption and "whitemailing" of politicians have only served to confirm the conclusion reached at the end of the poem.

Never Let Them Force You to Forget

Never let them
Force you to forget
How love
When true
Makes morning shine
How hope
When real
Gives strength
To rise and face them
One more time
No never let them
Force you to forget
There is no prison that
Can hold the human heart
No chains that can restrain
A freedom song
No cruelty, no suffering, no pain
Can silence truth—
And even death
Harsh death
They hurl down
From the skies
Cannot deny that
They are in decline, and
We are on the rise.

Drum Victory (from Cantos de Cuba)

Surely
With gentle touch
Rhythm
Begins
In Harmony.

Sunrise along the sea
Palm trees dancing leaves
Black sand blazing shore
We will be slaves no more.

Sunrise along the sea
Palm trees dancing leaves
Black sand flaming shore
We will make freedom roar.

Roar out across the seas
Work play victory
Our voices bursting free
Meet in mellow melody.

Roar out across the seas
Work play victory
Our souls bursting free
Hail a wild harmony.

The beat the heart
The sea to be free
The song revolution
The drum victory!

The drums play faster
Vibrating the earth
Message of happiness
The day is birth!

Beat heart
Roll sea
Spirit sing
Drum victory.

Surely
With gentle touch
Rhythm
Begins again
In Harmony.

Sunrise along the sea
Palm trees dancing leaves
Just peace on earth
The day drumming birth.

Sunrise along the sea
Palm trees dancing leaves
Beating on a drum
The revolution comes...

Cuba Si (from Cantos de Cuba)

Cuba
Si
Yanqui
No
Cuba
Afro-Latin
Island soul
Of continental revolution
Roll sea
Upon the shore
We shall be slaves no more
Soar winds
Around the changing globe
May more peoples
Careful, bold
Continue contributions
To new year's revolutions
Power grow
Cuba
Si
Yanqui
No!

The Land Is Life (from Cantos to Cuba)

The land is life
We shall win
From deep within
The harvest grows
Sustains our sustenance
Nourished by our labor
Joy and pain
Sugar cane
Tropical rain
Flows with the sweat and blood
Of those
Who work each day
Those who fought for freedom
In every necessary way
Land of strong sun
Our work has just begun
The sun beats heat
Upon the land is life
We shall win
From deep within
Our hearts
We know
The harvest grows
The martyrs bleed
Life flows
From conception to birth
As thought grows into deed
The human bends
Close to the earth
To plant
  the living
    seed...

The Night Before Moncada (from Cantos de Cuba)

The night before
The night before
The night before Moncada

How did you
Who were there
Prepare?

Did not fear
Rise inside your stomach
Spread to your head
With all the strength it gains
When you know
Tomorrow you may be dead?

The night before
The night before
The night before Moncada

Did not your eyes and mind
Perceive reality
With the immense intensity
Of the kind only freed
When human beings
Meet with historic destiny?

You were there
In Santiago secretly
In the restaurant
Eating with a few other comrades
Days of Carnival
Of masked costumed festivity
Days of Carnival
You were there
In Santiago secretly
Eating in the restaurant
At other tables
People sat and talked and laughed
The tree of liberty
Life moving on in Santiago
Good and evil
Hate and love
The sea below
The stars above

Santiago de Cuba
Life with a few who loan
Many who have to borrow
Life with all its joy
And sorrow
The other people
Eating in the restaurant
Did not know
What you would do tomorrow

How many
Maybe agents of Batista
Do you see
No it can't be
Fears about security
A cry a shout
Trying not to nervously
Look all about
The night before
The night before
What did you and your comrades
Talk about?

The night before
The night before
In a cheap hotel room
The next morning
Coming so soon
Sounds of Santiago night
Thin walls
Voices from the next room
Thin walls
Could not dilute
The argument between
A man and prostitute
On that night
What a heavy impression it made
The argument about
How much she should be paid
Slavery and sorrow
The other people
Did not know
What you would do tomorrow

The night before
The night before
The night before Moncada

Did not you wonder too
If it was
The wisest thing to do?

Doubts can't be
Blindly stamped out
Rather thought about
Analyzed and debated
Contingencies anticipated
Doubts can't be
Blindly stamped out
Rather thought about
Carefully struggled out

The people of our land
Live in misery
Degradation and corruption
Terror of tyranny
Listen to their cry
The people of this land
Shall surely rise

The revolutionary struggle
Is in the world
In Cuba and in Santiago
That is true
The revolutionary struggle
Also takes place
In you

It's not as though
You haven't thought it through before
It just gets more and more

You have agreed
To join freedom conspiracy
Because of so much
That you knew before
Your love for life and people
A comrade's grip
Your hatred of oppression
And this dictatorship

Perhaps a patriotic song
Or any unsung melody
Runs through your brain
What can be done
To prepare for pain
Perhaps some lines from
Revolutionaries of the past
The ones you love
The faces that you see
The tree of liberty
Your family
It's not as though
You haven't thought it through
Before
It just gets more and more
The future present and the past
At last
Another clear courageous inner light
Born of struggle
Resolves to do its best in freedom fight
It just gets more and more
Real people in real liberation war
The night before
The night before
The night before Moncada.

Note: This poem has been recited often on radio programs
and at community events commemorating the Cuban
Revolution. It is part of a larger work: "Cantos de Cuba." I
first visited Cuba as part of an "underground press" delega-
tion at the end of 1970 and start of 1971. It was a great trip,
included working alongside colleagues in the Cuban press,
visiting Santiago and other historic and beautiful sites,
learning about Radio Rebelde (the mountain guerrilla radio
station), and about the clandestine press during the Batista
dictatorship. We visited Moncada, which had been the
second largest fortress of the Batista tyranny. A primary
school was nearby, and the faces of the children shone with
the vital energy of a society where education and health care
are among the highest priorities, a society of hope and
promise.

The attack on Moncada, led by Fidel Castro in 1953, though a defeat, led to the growth of the movement that, six years later, overthrew Batista. In late 1973, just after the fascist coup in Chile, I again went to Cuba, with Gayle Markow, where we worked for a year in the English language department of Radio Havana Cuba, directed by a wonderful man who I'd met on the first trip, Guillermo Santiestaban. Among many experiences, I especially treasure my meeting with the great poet Nicolas Guillen, whose poetic content and rhythms brought African identity and Cuban music into poetry, much as his friend Langston Hughes wove the blues into his verse. Since then, I have heard many reports of the worsening of conditions in Cuba caused primarily by the imperialistic, idiotic, cruel, and hypocritical persistence of the U.S .government blockade against Cuba. Aware of the negative aspects of some facets of Cuban society, and no apologist for Soviet- or any style bureaucracy, I remain a firm supporter of the Cuban people's right to independence and am angered and saddened by the refusal of the US government to come to harmonious terms with this courageous people, whose cultural vitality is an Afro-Latin carnival of human freedom and creativity, even as the carnival in Cuba and many other nations has as one of its sources the one day off a year allowed by the slavemasters for celebration of African and indigenous cultures and spiritualities. ¡Cuba Si!

Guerrilla Couplets (from Cantos de Cuba)

Guerrilla sings draws dances plays a flute writes story essay verse
It is the people and their lives, not the guns, which must come first.

Guerrilla draws dances writes dreams plays a flute or sings
To be a revolutionary means to go deep into the roots of things.

Guerrilla draws dances plays flute sings writes verse preserves sanity
Learns that at the root of things is love for humanity.

Revolution is an art and you are all a vital part of it
Remember as you raise your fists it is the people who are the artists.

Song of Puerto Rico

To the rhythms of resistance
I heard a song arise
A song about an island
A nation colonized
Filled with pain and protest
Suffering and rage
Courage and defiance
Wild bird inside a cage
A history of struggle
Freedom banners blaze
Demanding independence
Fist from sea upraised

To the rhythms of resistance
I heard a song arise
A song about an island
A nation colonized
A people chant triumphant
Independence melody
A chorus through the branches
Of the palms of liberty.

Note: José Marti, the great Cuban independence leader, called Puerto Rico and Cuba two wings on the same bird of Freedom. I learned a lot about the valiant story of the Puerto Rican independence movement when I worked with a group of co-authors on the book *Puerto Rico: The Flame of Resistance*, published by People's Press. The book, now out of print, is an accessible narration of the island's history and national liberation movement. The Puerto Rican struggle is illuminated by the deeds and words of so many women and men—the courage of Lolita Lebron—the eloquence of Pedro Albizu Campos. Some of the political prisoners taken in this struggle have been released; others remain in prison. Under the colonial thumb of the Empire, the independence movement rose to mass revolutionary proportions several times in the 20th century and in the first years of the 21st has finally succeeded in forcing the U. S. Navy off the island of Vieques, where for many years it has conducted deadly and destructive bombing practice. ¡ Que Viva Puerto Rico Libre!

Confused and Mortal Beings (to Gayle)

I.
Confused and mortal beings, we
Will never know for sure what made
Those nights our nights,
The nights when merge-together
Was electrified with sudden love
When making love was making love
Not whistling in the dark
Nor the mechanics of pretense
But the real, the unforgettable
The authentic dance.

Confused and mortal beings, we
Were made together, unconfused,
Lay timeless. Nights when our minds
And bodies sang a rhythmed song of songs,
Nights of lightning flash, repeated sigh,
The freedom flashing in our eyes.

Those nights, when like a sailboat,
With its wings of love outspread
To embrace the wind, we found the
Current and the breeze, the sun, as
Bound together we set sail across
A widening expanse of waves which grew
So slowly and so certainly until
They gently, wildly washed upon the sand.
We held each other's hands and walked
Upon the surfing waves of love, then
Lay upon the sands again...again....again
We held so tight in every way
On those nights, our nights,
We sailed into the light of day.

Who cast that spell, did you or I,
As bewitched, we whispered in the wrinkled
Ear of time that it must halt to wait
For us, that what was yours was mine,
And mine was yours, the nights combine
To sing: We wrote a poem, the two of us
Our minds and bodies were the rhyme.

II.
Time passes and the day must come
When parting sings its ragged blues
Internal worlds meet worlds outside,
But what we've had can never be erased.
Look back in happiness and not in tears,
Look back but look ahead, for years, like
Waves are stretched before you and memories
Build newer poems, new days, life full of sun
Look far ahead for much has just begun.

The darkest hour just before the dawn, for
Men and women and for the times in which they live.
Walk beautifully, beautiful, go well,
Make of the strength and love we showed
New smiles to lessen loads, to bless,
Go well, make of our poems and of our time
A bridge to bells that chime your happiness.

In the Valley of Viñales

"A just cause from the depths of a cave
Can do more than an Army…"

—José Marti

In the valley of Viñales
Where the palms with pine trees grow
And the hills rise strange and sudden
From green valley floor below

We have been there we have seen it
We have marvelled at the view
In the valley of Viñales
There is love of me and you

Many are the paths we've travelled
On the winding way of love
Over mountains into valleys
With the Cuban clouds above

Winding like a river
Cutting caves through mountain stone
Struggling through the barriers
Knowing we are not alone

From where love sends out its signals,
Transmits its strong señales
May your life be filled with gladness
Your pain be blessed by solace

As we view our lives before us
Like the valley of Viñales…

Note: This poem, slightly edited for this collection, originally
had 27 lines and was written for Gayle Markow on her 27th
birthday. It springs from our visit, during our year in Cuba,
to the valley of Viñales, an awesome area in Cuba, where
unusual hills, buttes, and strangely-shaped earth formations
rise up oddly and suddenly, covered in tropical green, in a
unique geology.

Red Curtains (January, 1977)

The red curtains on the clothesline
Look beautiful
Shining in the morning sun:
A bright hope
Dancing in the wind.

Soon they will brighten
Our new room
Look out on a new street
Open and close, breathing in rhythm
With the day and night.

Red curtains
On the windows of our lives
Bright hope
Shining in the morning sun.

Kinder Gentler Rock-A-Byes

Rock-a-bye baby
In the tree top
When the wind blows
The cradle will rock
When the sun shines
The baby will smile
And she'll go to sleep
After a while.

Rock-a-bye baby
In the tree top
When the wind blows
The cradle will rock
When the birds sing
The baby will rise
To look on the world with
Love in her eyes.

Rock-a-bye baby
In the tree top
When the wind blows
The cradle will rock
When the birds sing
The baby will sway
Dancing along with
A beautiful day.

Passover 1977

Everything is expectancy,
A becoming, changing constantly,
Full moon,
Soon to be eclipsed,
Child inside, crouching to be born,
Everything is expectancy,
And freedom
Freedom triumphs over slavery,
Love fills the eyes with tears of joy.

Time for commemoration
Time for celebration:
Why is this day different from all other days?
And the angel of death passed over,
Save a seat for the Prophet Elijah,
Red sea of revolution opening
To let the ships of struggle through,
Does it seem as though we wander in circles
For years and years, well, that's because we do.
But we do not wander aimlessly because
Our eyes are fixed on freedom
And life springs forth once more anew,
For lo—the winter is past
The song of the turtle is heard in our land!

Yes, an affirmation,
Even amidst imperial decay,
Yes, a celebration—
It's not what rituals or words we say,
But what is really in
Our hearts and minds and stomachs
That binds us together.

As always
The bread is unleavened
Yet our spirits rise like yeast
Passover 1977
Within the belly of the beast.

Anna's Birth Announcement

Out of the earth, our mother of mothers
Churning up into wheat, rice, and corn
Life leaps into being with all of its power
After long labor a new child is born!!!

      Anna Thai Binh
      Born August 2nd, 1977
      To Gayle and Lincoln

      Alert and mellow, sucking strong
      Eight pounds four ounces,
      Twenty-one inches long.

      In Vietnamese
      Her middle name
      Means hard-won peace.

      Hosannas of welcome
      In chorus begin:
      Welcome sweet Anna, Anna Thai Binh!

Out of the earth, our mother of mothers
Churning up into wheat, rice, and corn
Life leaps into being with all of its power
After long labor a new child is born!!!

This Is A Proofreader

Eyes tired, yet still concentrating,
Straining to swoop down and catch mistakes,
Like an owl upon a rodent,
This is our very own proofreader, one of a vanishing species.

Although this one has been known
To miss some fairly large and costly errors
We will probably let him stay on—
He plays a half-decent game of ping-pong
And is the one who washes out the coffee grounds.

So this, ladies and gentlemen,
Is a genuine proofreader —
Please note the shifty eyes, the stooped shoulders,
The defensive, pugnacious tone.

Have pity on the poor proofreader
Just imagine his sad plight—those sleepless nights
When his eyes refuse to close, and just go
Back and forth and to and fro
Like an upbeat ping-pong pendulum.

Our zoo is very pleased
To have acquired this fine specimen
Please humor him, as he, like all of us,
Has a distinct and fierce hatred of captivity.

Note: This poem is based on my five-year experience as a union
proofreader (last of a dying breed) at a large metropolitan
printing company. Despite tedium and speedup, the pay was
OK, and my co-workers, artists and typesetters, were good to
hang with—every day at lunch we played intense ping pong
games. Given that some of the proofreading involved internal
procedural manuals of the phone company, I was definitely
paying some dues! It helped to recall that my mother was a
proofreader for the St. Paul, Minnesota newspapers and then
for the Bancroft-Whitney law publishing firm. I remember her
exultation at finding errors. This job perhaps helped me pay
some homage to her, besides being the first one I could manage
to get after coming back from Cuba to a much less open Bay
Area media scene. The format of this poem is modeled after a
series of wonderful poetic vignettes by the great Afro-Cuban
poet Nicolas Guillen who I had the honor to meet and talk with,
a friend of Langston Hughes and Pablo Neruda, from a series
Nicolas Guillen called "The Human Zoo."

On Reading a Speech to a Meeting

Your words leapt out at me
With all their careful dedication
Words we had been waiting for...

One time I was in jail for 30 days
A Black prisoner
Ravaged by heroin
Yet still possessed
Of wisdom and a ready wit, told me:
"Class tells, shit smells, and water seeks its own level."

Words I never forgot
Because class does tell
And it is this recognition
That marks the transition from
Radical courage to revolution.

My fellow prisoner also told me:
"Yeh, Linc, the meek shall inherit the earth—
all six feet of it!"

Your words leapt out at me
A different emotion
From when I was a child
And heard the words to workers' songs like:
Joe Hill, Union Maid, Song of the United Front, or
Which Side Are You On?

A different emotion
But the same sensation
That here at last
May be the unity we seek
(Not of the meek)
So, to many more meetings,
Speak sister speak!

Love Changes: Sonnet Amply Plagiarized (1973)

Love is love which changes with our changes:
Does not cold winter struggle into spring?
So from woe to happiness love ranges
Bare ruinéd choirs yet still the sweet birds sing.
Some say that love remains an ever-fixéd mark
A beauty frozen for eternity
Yet fire begins with just a single spark
And raging rivers flow into the sea.
Love as an art rejects no part of life
Change pulses with the throbbing of our hearts
Serenity is born out of great strife
As yet another contradiction starts.

If love can face despair and struggle know
It may exist and it can even grow.

Note: This sonnet is a play on one of Shakespeare's (the one
that begins "Love is not love which alters when it alteration
finds/O no, it is an ever-fixed mark..."). One of the finest
teachers I ever had, Warren Carrier, who taught literature in
a wonderfully experiential and memorable way, took issue
with Shakespeare's sentiment and began his own response
with a powerful line I have appropriated: "Love is love
which changes with our changes." Shakespeare's original
and lines from other sonnets of his are freely quoted after
that and, to complete the grand theft, the last couplet is
taken from one of my father's most moving love poems.

Optimistic Shakespeare

Tomorrow and tomorrow and tomorrow
Leaps in sweet embrace from day to day
And all our yesterdays
Have truly lighted ways
To better times
Shine shine bright candle
Life is far more than shadow
Brave beings who whirl and spin
Their hours upon the stage
As crowds call out for more
It is a tale told by each of us
Full of struggle and beauty
Signifying everything.

Sonnet on Writing

Each single word is like a child in birth
Each sentence is a newborn infant's cry
Each paragraph a hymn to human worth —
Each chapter sings a loving lullaby.
And like the labor leading to the child
The work is hard and sorely strains
Draft after draft is circularly filed
Emotions flare and mad confusion reigns
Yet from such *sturm* and *drang* may yet emerge
A precious thing upon which people look
With much appreciation, magic merge
Of human meaning that we call a book.

Although my labors endless seem to be
I'll hold on to my hopes in poetry.

Sonnet on Friendship

When I consider how our lives are spent,
Our comings and our goings ebb and flow,
Yes, when I sadly ponder where it went,
Those facts forgotten that I used to know,
The times sped by, so fleeting and so sweet,
Courageous chants of liberty unfurled
That demonstrating beat of marching feet
Resounding music all around the world.
Today we listen to more sombre chords—
Is joyous unity just sad illusion?
As we divide they sharpen up their swords,
Yet all of earth cries out for retribution.

For that sweet day when all oppression ends
I send this poem with love to all true friends.

Note: This sonnet was sent out in gratitude to friends of my
father and myself who had helped put together a small
collection of his poems entitled *Will We Remember?* The book
was printed in a small limited edition in Chicago by several of
his closest comrades there and was used to raise funds for his
medical care. In its introduction, I briefly trace some of our
family story alongside my father's revolutionary trajectory.

Happy Birthday to Joe from Lincoln

Friendship
Like a flower
Can be fragile
Yet its roots can
Crack through stone
Friendship hangs on
During dry spells
Can weather storms
Sometimes I think that
Friendship is the strongest power known

So my friend
As river time
Keeps rolling
Round the bend
As you reach
Two score four
I wish you many more

Our
Friendship
Like a pear
When nurtured
With care
Shall
Survive
And thrive
For Love is at the core.

Sonnet to Dorth and Will
on their 40th Anniversary

To stay together wed is no mean feat
It is composed of kind and giving deeds
The sun's not always found on Marriage Street
Love's flowers often overrun by weeds.
Yet through it all these two have walked along
Through difficulty, anguish, weals and woes
Perhaps because they walked on wings of song
While warmth of laughter melted sorrow's snows.
A dedicated struggle set the stage
And though frustration wrinkled Freedom's brow
The book of Family, writ page by page
Is living testament to then and now.
These lines of Love are all I have to greet
This joyous celebration—no mean feat!

Birthday Sonnet to Dorothy   February 1990

Another's heart, says she, is forest dark,
The mysteries of life so oft unseen,
Yet in her leaps an understanding spark
That casts its light upon the shadowed scene.
Illumination to awake the child,
Whom others call impossible to teach,
Abandoned sombre spirits are beguiled,
Her giving strength brings competence in reach.

Once daily shook by subway's clash and clang,
She now returns to waters called sky blue,
Beneath those boughs where late the sweet birds sang,
She and her Will to love and struggle true.
From heart to heart my poetry shines forth
A birthday sonnet with my love to Dorth.

Sonnet for Wilbur Strong Broms   (July 8, 1990)

A high sweet voice that soared so clear and strong
Beloved comradeship that does not fade
In opera or Irish freedom song
The Internationale or Union Maid.
Repression's wind blew hard and bitter cold
The hounds of Hell seemed always at your heels,
You and your songs could not be bought and sold
Rang out for justice, damned their dirty deals.
The rising of the peoples round the earth
Is power greater than all hoarded gold,
Your voice affirms a better world in birth
Wherein your life and stories shall be told.
Your songs shall never sound in slavery
And will live on as all the Earth breathes free.

Note: This poem was read at a memorial for my uncle Wilbur Broms before we played a recording of his pure tenor singing the Irish revolutionary song "The Minstrel Boy." I helped emcee the ceremony, and before reciting the poem said: "I offer this sonnet, dedicated to Wilbur, with all my love and utmost respect to Dorothy, and to Pat and Martin, and all that our families have shared together." Wilbur was the son of two extraordinary radicals, Alan and Claire Broms. Alan was a working class intellectual and scientist extraordinaire, who set up and taught at worker's schools, and whose book and theory of the expanding universe was way ahead of its time. Claire was a firebrand who was a member of the Industrial Workers of the World (IWW) and a founding member of the U.S. Communist Party. Wilbur grew up radical, working class, and Irish in Minnesota. He had a wonderful tenor voice and became a fine opera singer, singing with the NBC Symphony Orchestra and, after serving in the infantry in Europe during World War II, was moving upward at the New York Metropolitan Opera when the repression of the early 1950s hit and he was "whitelisted." His beautiful renditions of "The Minstrel Boy," "Kevin Barry," and other Irish revolutionary and popular songs are among my most treasured memories. He continued performing at small concerts, did intense organizing around schools and other issues in New York, wrote a massive unpublished book on the great Irish poet and patriot Thomas Moore, and remained devoted to the cause, but was often saddened and frustrated. I was fortunate to interview him in depth on his life and background, and on the relation of art and politics, and that interview resides in the Minnesota Historical Society's collection of the many Minnesotans who dedicated their lives to social change.

Sonnet for My Mother

Image returns in waves of tenderness
I see your face as in a moonglow light,
I see your curly hair, your simple dress,
Your shadow bending over me at night.
I know you had your failings, faults, and fears,
Some dreams unrealized, regret and doubt,
Yet when I travel back to those green years,
It doesn't take me long to figure out
That over-arching all the memories
In shining rainbow aura high above
There is one sacred thing you gave to me:
A sense of what it means to truly love.

Dear Ma, though cancer took your flesh and bone,
Your children know that they are not alone.

Sonnet
(with meter variation)

The day will come when age will dull my brain
When movements I now do with ease
Will take worse toll of ache and pain
Till then my deepest sentiments are these:

To thine own self be true remains as apt
As ever was and ever be
When reservoirs of self are tapped
Such knowledge holds the key to destiny.

Follow your heart they say in sweet cliché
As if the path ahead were clear
Yet hard to find your heart's own way
To overcome the manacles of fear.

To reach this place you live as best you can
Love's learning crammed into a lifetime's span.

To Hold Your Body

To hold your body warm against my own
May be perhaps the greatest good of all,
When even eagle ecstasy has flown,
In whose empowered wings we rise and fall—
Long after that climactic energy
There is another kind of tenderness
Triumphant over pain, despair, ennui,
The closest we can come to happiness.

I chant the reaching touching holding need
The human urge to sense serenity
The infant nuzzling, seeking breast to feed,
Connection to creation's mystery.

The act itself can sing, bring great release,
Yet warm embrace begets more lasting peace.

Auto-Immune Deficiency Blues

Woke up this mornin', heard another one done gone
Woke up this mornin', heard another one done gone
Got to run for shelter, got to pray to meet the dawn.

Plague done took 'em, plague that they call AIDS
Plague done took them, disease that they call AIDS
Biologic bullet, virus sharp as razor blades.

To be "positive" these days is a sad and mournful tune
Bein' "positive" these days sings a sad and mournful tune
And from this deadly virus—no one living is immune.

Time we shouted "fire!" in this crowded theatre
'Bout time we shouted "fire!" in Earth's crowded theatre
Get our heads together and come up with a cure.

Woke up this mornin', heard one more to AIDS had gone
Woke up this mornin', heard another soul done gone
That's when I decided that I had to write this song.

Written On the First Night
of the Israeli Invasion of Lebanon   June 1982

Tonight
My Jewish soul
Weeps in Lebanon

    For the child of Palestine
    Her ragged corpse
    Strewn among the wreckage
    Of Israeli bombing raids.

Tonight
My Jewish heart
Beats in Lebanon

    Pulses to sustain
    Against all odds
    The struggle for justice
    In Palestine
    Pulses in affirmation
    Of a people's right
    To self-determination.

Tonight
The full moon shines
But in Lebanon
Her light
Sheds no serenity
Upon the cedars
Instead the moon
Looks down upon
A blood-soaked tragedy
Glows fluorescent
Upon the crimson streams
The night is shattered
By the ceaseless screams.

Tonight
My holocaustal soul
Flies to Lebanon

Because
No matter
Whatever pretense
No matter
The attempted disguise
The big lies
Begin calls it
One of the noblest military endeavors
In history
But no matter
The Pharisee robes of hypocrisy
Behind which these invaders hide
The ceaseless scream
Of Lebanon
Is genocide.

Tonight
My Warsaw Ghetto heart
Leaps to Lebanon

There to resist
To chant
To sing as
Ghetto warriors sang:

"Never say that you have reached
The very end
Though leaden skies
A bitter future may portend
Because the hour for which we yearned
Will yet arrive
And our marching steps will thunder
We survive!"

A song to remind us
With unyielding persistence
Wherever oppression
There resistance.

Tonight
My Elijah spirit
Soars to Lebanon

To be as one
With the exile, the lost
The dispossessed
The homeless
War-torn, tempest-tossed

Elijah the Prophet
Sometimes known too
As the Wandering Jew
Wends his way
So sorrowfully
Through the carnage
Perpetrated by those
Who falsely claim
Elijah as their own:

Now let it be forever known
Yet shall be reaped what has been sown

For Elijah always
Walks along with the oppressed
Identifies with all of us
Who cherish freedom
Each who believe
That lasting peace
Can only be achieved
When it is based
On Justice and Equality

Elijah the Prophet
In this time
A citizen of
Emerging Palestine
Shouting in protest
Crouching on the barricades

Saying
       Let my people go!
       Praying
       Lord this hurts so bad
       Is there no balm in Gilead?

Elijah the Prophet
Raising his staff
Anger blistering
He tears his hair
Then let the strutting kings
Of Zion in Lebanon beware
For the Prophet Elijah
Is also buried there

Yes, it is true
When they lift their sword
Against the people
Of Lebanon and Palestine
They kill Elijah too

Now let it be forever known
Yet shall be reaped what has been sown
We cannot let them fight alone

Just as David
Huge Goliath slew
So when
Elijah of Palestine
Rises reborn
Justice will have her due.

And that is why
Tonight
My human heart and soul and mind
Are intertwined
With Lebanon

This human spirit
That is mine
Casts its lot
With Palestine.

Blues for Beirut

(September 21, 1982)

Got those blues in the mornin'
Blues in the night
Blues when we're lovin'
Blues when we fight
Blues when I'm sleepin'
Blues when I wake
Blues when I'm givin'
Blues when I take
Blues when I'm lyin'
Or tellin' the truth
Blues like I'm dyin'
Those blues..........for Beirut.

Got those blues in my breakfast
Blues for my lunch
Blues served for dinner
Blue Sunday brunch
Blues when I'm workin'
Blues when I play
Blues when I'm singin'
Blues when I pray
Blues when I'm laughin'
Or takin' a toot
Blues like I'm dyin'
Those blues..............for Beirut.

From blues of a bluebird
To blues of the sky
Blues of the ocean
Blues of goodbye
Blues of deep purple
Blues of blood red
Blues of the world
Goin' out of its head
Blues when I'm cryin'
Blues when they shoot
Blues like I'm dyin'
Those blues..........for Beirut.

Mantra Contra Contras

Mantra contra contras
One hundred million more
Mantra contra contras
Rotten to the core
Millions more for murder
More to rape and maim
Millions more to contras
To buy and sell cocaine
One hundred million more
Is much more than a shame
It is a crime of war
As World Court did decide
Illegal and immoral
An act of genocide
Congress pulls the trigger
Nicaraguan children die
Mantra contra contras
Imperial big lies
Yet Colossus of the North
Will be cut down to size
Nicaraguan people
Sandino in their eyes
Rise to meet the challenge
The world is on their side
Mantra contra contras
For the day when we shall see
The contras and their bosses
Rot in infamy.

Haiku for John Santos

Hand spin
Drum skin
In rhythm true—
¡ Santos Espiritú !

The Contragate Rap (May 19, 1987)

Call it Contragate, call it Iranscam
Call it anything but what it am
Call North a hero, better dead than red,
I call him villain, that's what I said,
Call it Iranscam, call it Contragate
But if what it is was served on your plate
You'd take one whiff and get downright sick
Cause the you-know-what's spread on so thick
I just can't stand it, this stench so rank
Of millions for slaughter in some Swiss bank
Of millions for contras, drug-dealing thugs
Crawling the earth like blood-sucking bugs
Millions to murder, millions to rape,
Call it Iranscam, call it Contragate,
It is blood for profit, it is fear and hate,
The seamiest of affairs of state
Call it any clever or catchy name—
But the truth will always remain the same
They may strut and boast but they can't hide
They stand convicted of genocide.
They stand convicted, you heard me jack
And don't try to tell me to take it back
I know these jackals, mad dogs of war,
Violently vicious down to the core,
They foam at the mouth and seethe inside,
Tighten their jaws in macho pride
From GI Joe to Rambo Ron
It is a death trip they are on
Like vultures circling over the dead
Their weapons race is based on dread
As they test the bombs, and point their guns,
It seems to me that Attila's huns
Pale beside these arrogant bums
Who trample on laws, and Congress too
But mostly vamp on me and you.

There's one big thing to understand
Something's going on in that bright land
Hey—Nicaragua's rising free
If ya don't believe me go and see
There's lots of problems and some mistakes
But so much more of what it takes
To bring a people out from the past
Into a future that just might last
With hope and hospitals and schools
Reading and writing and all the tools
To build up out of poverty
After hundreds of years of misery.

There's something else I've got to say
Cuz something happened the other day
That made me shake my head again
It had to do with a man named Ben
Twenty-seven years old, hailed from San Fran
Here was a truly remarkable man
Benjamin Linder, a really great guy,
A brave engineer with joy in his eye,
Electrical expert, a juggler and clown,
Bringing new power to each little town,
Now here is somebody who did what was right
Gave of his gifts to let there be light
Gave Nicaragua many years and his life
Working despite all the danger and strife
Yet those murdering contras shot Ben Linder down
At point-blank range blasted him to the ground
Now here is a hero well worth the name
Here is a man who was not after fame
Who would quickly remind us how many have died
I'll say it again—it is sheer genocide.
Remember Ben Linder—the song of his spirit
Lives on in the lives of all who can hear it,
And as for who should be charged with this crime
Just follow the logic expressed in my rhyme

Don't get distracted—go right to the top
Right to the place where the bloody bucks stop

Into the White House, the master suite,
Of Ronald the Raygun, with Bush at his feet,
Deceased William Casey, McFarland, and Meese,
The entire grim gaggle of carnivorous geese
Weinberger's a weasel, Schultz is a snake,
And Howard Baker's a man on the make,
Poindexter and Secord, the list grows and grows
As does the length of Ronnochio's nose
To draw a conclusion who needs a speech
It all can be said in that one word "impeach!"
But meanwhile the Congress, plodding and meek,
Is giving these madmen much room to speak,
Today one of their henchman recited a poem
Oh to what depths has poetry blown—
A lyrical tribute to Blood and Guts North
Who did Ronald's bidding, adventuring forth,
To take over the government, put law on the shelf,
In what we'd call "coup" were it anywhere else.

What else can I say—I'm at my wit's end
Maybe I'll go talk it out with a friend
This whole controversy comes down to one theme
The cauldron is boiling but beyond all the steam
Contradictions are rising, becoming intense
There's only one thing that makes any sense
Get rid of this pirate and his whole bloody crew
End all aid to the contras—make peace with the new

Send signals of friendship from here to Managua
Repair the war wounds throughout Nicaragua
Let the people decide, let us all work for peace
Then and then only will this madness cease
Remember Ben Linder—Remember him well
His spirit will dance to liberty's bell
Remember Ben Linder—Remember him well
His spirit will dance to liberty's bell
His spirit will dance to liberty's bell.....

Note: Performed on KPFA-FM in Berkeley with me doing the
"rap" and world-renowned percussionist and musicologist
John Santos on congas, produced by my longtime close
friend and radio co-producer Emiliano Echeverria.

Sonnet for South Africa

I long to live to see that day's bright dawn
When this brave dream so long deferred comes true
When even vile apartheid's stench is gone
As people stride down Biko Avenue.
I see Mandela's daughter standing strong
Eyes smiling with that shining struggle light
I hear the universal freedom song
Yet feel the chains of bondage pressing tight.
May millions still enslaved be strengthened by
Harriet Tubman's courage and her rage
May we who witness this do more than cry
Do what we can to help to turn the page.

Great chapter in the book of liberty
The day Azania at last is free!

Just After Ides of March 1985

I. Coming to My Senses

Coming to my senses I realized
That what I wanted to do was precisely that:
To come to my senses again—
To look out upon the world
With the wonder of a child.
To open up my ears and eyes
And nose and mouth,
Reach out and touch somebody's hand.
Coming to my senses I realized...

But am I really coming to my senses?
Have I been acting crazily?
Am I just pretending to be better?
Does anyone really know
How much I hurt inside?
No worse nor better I know
Than any other suffering soul
We all suffer in one way or another
All have our crosses to bear
So the upshot is I do not really know
Whether or not I am coming to my senses
Or if I really want to do so.
Still, feeling as if I might be
Coming to my senses at long last
I thought I'd write this poem
To capture that moment just before
A person comes to their senses
On the off chance that this time
Just maybe I might actually be
Coming to my senses, and if not
Consider this merely another entry
In the diary of my sad and searching self.

II. All the Things I've Done

All the things I've done and all I've yet to do
Somehow fade from me this morning
As I wake with pain inside me, no one beside me,
Wondering if my present impasse will ever end
Feeling discouraged, suicidal, lost at sea,
Abandoned like a raft, tempest-tossed,
Breaking apart, barely managing to stay afloat.
Where is the strength, energy, and motivation
I remember having, that I gave of so generously
As Stevie Wonder sang, where is my spirit,
I'm nowhere near it—where is that *joie de vivre*
That lusty, laughing, sexy man, that voice
Of poetry, that winding horn of healing music
Where has it gone? All the things I've done—
Let's hope and pray the things I've yet to do
Will help to bring me out of this morass,
Quicksand made of my own doubts and fears
Lacks of self esteem. I look at others
With their smiles and happiness, know of course
That everyone doubts their own worth, but still and all
I just can't seem to shake this feeling—is it
The original abandonment that lays me low?
From the abandonment of my mother's death
To the abandonment of making love
Perhaps that is the road to hoe, a way to go,
I really do not know—and on that note
I guess I'll close this rather aimless entry
The second in this journal of my battered soul.

III. Sometimes My Mind Returns

Sometimes my mind returns upon my checkered past
In unbelieving awe at risks and chances scattered in my path
Somehow I made it through, and yet today I must
Reflect upon the pain that I internalized along the way
Death and disease, rejection and misused kindness,
Had I been more fully able to express my grief and anger
I would not be in this hard place today, would perhaps
Have been more able to curtail losses, consolidate gains.
Meanwhile, I once more, due to a cold, dodge taping
A radio show, but the impulses seem to be there again.
Next week, the Spanish Civil War commemoration,
I feel my voice returning, sense the truth
Of the creative chakra being in the throat.
Bell's palsy all too slowly eases—I can almost play my horn.

This deep internal struggle keeps going on and on
Preventing me from speaking out with that old strength
Yearning for new, more vital powers, trying hard to change
Meanwhile, so many shot down in South Africa and Lebanon.

Beardless and entering Spring
I pray for a new lease on Life, an Opening!

Note: A new lease on life indeed. The three previous poems
and others in this time frame reflect a period of separation
and loss in close relationships, mid-life crisis, disorientation
after leaving a long time editorial position, mourning for the
social ease and warm, more trusting connections between
people that were so much a part of life during heydays of the
radical social and cultural movements. For nine months I
lived in a mortuary apartment on Dolores Street. The
sadness, depression, and despair were there, but so also
were the seeds of a new sense of myself, a more personal
sense of poetry, and much appreciation for those who helped
me through into the next stage. While I had nothing directly
to do with the mortuary, the elevator went up and down
with the inexorability of death, and once the manager asked
me to pick up the hearse from an auto repair shop.

Driving the Hearse

Driving the hearse
Through San Francisco streets
Nice old black Cadillac
A few curious stares
But mostly rush-hour madness
Still there was a sense of power—
Other drivers give
A hearse a wide berth.

I thoroughly enjoyed the drive
A new experience
Some sort of thrill
Is this perverse?
Could be—but I ask you
Which is worse:
To be tied down by depression
Or drive a hearse?

To die is neither
Blessing nor curse
I had a good time today
Driving that hearse...

I See Such Sadness

I SEE SUCH SADNESS IN MY FACE
I SEE IT ETCHED LIKE NERUDA'S SOMETIMES SEEMED
IN DEEP CREVICES OF PAIN LIKE
A SHARD OF GRANITE STUCK INTO MY GUTS
SCRAPING ALONG MY HIP
LURKING LIKE A DEMON IN MY LEFT TESTICLE
I HATE THIS PAIN I HAVE
I WANT TO DEFEAT IT
TO DRIVE IT OUT FROM MY BODY
TO SET MYSELF FREE
FROM THIS CONSTANT SENSE
OF SOMETHING BEING WRONG
I SCREAM OUT LOUD, LOOKING IN THE MIRROR:
"I HATE I HATE I HATE -- I HATE THIS PAIN!"

Naked at the Macintosh Computer

Naked at the Macintosh computer
I listen to Rachmanioff
And then to John Coltrane
People tell me it seems like
Computers and poetry do not mix
But I've found out just the opposite:

So far I've found this particular computer
Conducive to poetry, very flowing, visual,
Instantly changeable, before your very eyes,
In a number of type designs, or fonts,
As well as various type styles and sizes,
Not to mention you can draw on it
And all can be printed exactly as you wish

It just might be that this sort
Of modern writing machine will become
A great liberator of the poetic impulse
Found in all human beings—leading to
Some new techniques and tools for
The construction of the House of Poetry.

The foundation always has to be
Our Great Mother Earth, the sun and stars
Redwood tree, seahorse, duckbill platypus,
The very spirit of life itself—the
Opening vocal chords of human beings,
Their search for creative expression,
A way to say— "hey, what it is?"
And "what it be" is poetry...

Conceived, nourished, protected, and carried
Getting heavier, starting to wiggle, to kick,
Those tiny hands, those teenzy-weenzy toes—
What it be is poetry coming into birth
What it be is you and me and the entire Earth.
Poetry is sweet music
The flute playing of
A young woman

Reclining on a grassy hillside
Hauntingly romantic
Melodic rhapsody
In harmony with the wildflowers
Her dress far from fancy
Hand-sewn, well-worn
Her feet bare, her eyes cast upward
Deciphering the messages of clouds

Poetry is a drum
A different drummer
Signals exchanged between tribes
A call to battle
A steady pulsing rhythm of daily life
Birth and death, love and work.
As Nina Simone sings:
"It ain't as simple as talkin' jive
The daily struggle just to stay alive..."

Poetry is the saxophone
In ensemble or all alone
As in John Coltrane or Charles Parker
Or the slide trombone, the piccolo,
The instruments of wind and string
The open-throated bird—so sing
Lift every voice, let freedom ring!

Billie isn't gone
She's just on holiday...
Along with Bessie Smith
Poetry's a wailing ambulance
Along a lonesome highway
A chain gang chant, a secret code
Along an underground railroad, running
In the direction signaled by
The Drinkin' Gourd up in the sky.
Poetry's a child that's got her own
A jump-rope rhyme
In the patchwork quilt of history
A poem is a stitch in time

And time, flowing in rivers to the sea,
Begins in underwater aquifers and springs
In rivulets where lilies grow
Lotuses emerge, tadpoles swim
In time, pouring down in monsoon rains
Thundering, electrifying sky,
Time rains down, and in this moment I
Look out my window, see
The falling rain, in my mind's eye
I see your face and hear again the sad refrain
Since you went away the days grow long
And soon I'll hear old winter's song...
But I miss you most of all, my darling,
When autumn leaves start to fall—it's then I see
My mother's face imprismed in my tears
Poetry is mother-child
Poetry is tender, wild
Feeling, loving, touching, holding,
Missing, kissing, and enfolding
Poetry—I see her face
Poetry is passionate embrace
Peaceful, meditative, and serene
Moonlight on the lapping stream
Free vistas wide, to break the bars,
To gaze in wonder at the stars.

Poetry is a planting, a tending
A gardening, a harvesting, a gathering
African violet, opening orchid
Dandelion dancing in the breeze
A green thumb for poetry brings forth
Amazing blossoming—I see her face
Such grace was in her shining spirit
Such light shone in her eyes, poetry
Running red in my veins
Beating in my heart
Treasures my pleasures
Measures my pains
So may poetry evoke the spirit
Bring me near it, help me hear it

For these are the poems of my heart
Offered not to display their art
But to express that part of me
Mortally wounded with her physical death
And now aching to be reborn
To open up that part of her
That lives in me—unchain my heart
Set me free, to free the soul of poetry
To bring forth my own blossoming
Upon ancestral family tree.

These poems are not words on paper
They are a part of me
In the flesh, forty years old,
Getting into better shape, I have a
Small brown mole on the tip of my nose.
Actually, if you look at it closely
It has a bluish tinge,
And doctors call it a blue nevus.
It grew on me during puberty—
The most important thing about it
Is something the children know
If you press the dot on my nose
It will beep, with this proviso—
THE SOFTER YOU PRESS IT
THE LOUDER IT BEEPS.
Also, it gets tired after several beeps,
Depending on the circumstances
Although it has been known to
Go on for quite a while
And usually it brings a smile
There's no doubt
The mole on the end of my nose
Is a distinctive part of me
So, indubitably, is my poetry!

Sunday Morning

Sunday morning in the mortuary
Just after 5 AM
In a few hours people and cars will descend
Upon this corner, 16th and Dolores
Parking wherever they can
To attend church—to offer prayers and psalms
To an imagined God, an imaged deity.
Dressed in beautiful yet modest dresses
In somewhat sombre suits, conservative ties
Listening to a priest or other religious leader
Intone the lessons of the Bible
Call forth the life of Jesus Christ once more
Sunday morning in the mortuary
A few blocks away, as night begins to die,
The moon reveals a woman men call whore
So young, so drugged, so desperate
For just a little more before the Sunday morning
Comes—cars still careen along the streets
A siren here, a screech of brakes, a distant scream
I do not know how many dead bodies are here tonight
I do know that I am happy to be alive
My daughter, a wonderful inquisitive, always learning
Seven year old, says, only half-jokingly,
That she'll sleep here if I can guarantee
There will be no ghosts and no skeletons
So far, I haven't made the acquaintance of any
Though there must be many—as for
Skeletons in the closet of humanity, that
Is an entire story in and of itself—

Hardly told, it already fills
Each and every shelf, sends
Sound waves of classical music
Of rhythm and blues
Of African lullabies and freedom chants
Cuban sons, Brazilian sambas
Haunting Middle Eastern melodies
Ringing Asiatic reveries
Gregorian chants and Muslim prayers
The Druids singing, dancing
All around what we now call
The Stonehenge monument

Sending upward to the galaxies
Resounding in the firmament
All the music, poetry, the sounds of play
Of laughter and of joy
The sounds of making love
Mixing so tragically with the
Maddening saddening roar of war
The living skeletons of famine
The dispossessed and homeless
Of this planet, populated
By so many intricate and vital species
Including one capable of
Creating works of incredible beauty
Of sending Coltrane as a gift to the Universe
But afflicted by a self-inflicted cruelty
And now also capable of causing
The total destruction of this good green Earth
This Mother who nourishes us all

Such were my thoughts
Very early Sunday morning in the mortuary
The place I now call home
And where I evolve this poem—
Dylan Thomas, born on the same day as I,
Speaks of pulsing life— "the force that through
The green fuse drives the flower,"
So may these words have power

May they echo in the coffin-lined hallways
As do these courageous lines of my poet-birthmate
"Do not go gently into that good night
Rage rage against the dying of the light."
May the mortician's operating room and surgical table
Be overshadowed by irreverent poet's rhyme and fable
And Death Shall Have No Dominion.
May life be affirmed and celebrated
Held on to, embraced, and treasured
On this Sunday morning in the mortuary
Even as the lovers intertwine in ecstasy
Joining together in sensual desire
Thus Andrew Marvell described the urgency:
"At my back I always hear
Time's wingéd chariot drawing near"

And, when it came to seizing time for loving
He said it like it is:
"The grave's a fine and private place
But none I think do there embrace"
And so this morning
With the arms and legs of poetry
I encircle the entire earth
With petitions for peace
With protests against oppression
This Sunday morning
The spirits of all ancestors
Are harbored in my heart
Like resistant slaves
Finding refuge in a safe house
Along the Underground Railway
Not ghosts or skeletons
Or any Halloween imaginings
These spirits sing in choruses
Of billions, a church choir
A great and growing gospel song
The day now dawns—still one more
Sunday morning, November 11, 1984.

Sunday morning in the mortuary
The sunlight spreads an apricot-peach glow
Arising from the cradle of the eastern sky—
Shining dawning light of new day's birth
Above the vast, foreboding dark gray clouds
Surmounting the storm—bursting free
To bring forth life-giving heat and energy
No wonder ancient religions worshipped the Sun
Made gods of nature and the Universe
Made sacred offerings to our Mother Earth.

And so today, amidst the tumult and the fears
As I now enter what they call "middle" years
I too will pray, for that precious, so elusive
Worldwide blending of justice and serenity
A prayer responded to recently
By the poet-leader-priests of Nicaragua
And, in their turn, by dedicated thousands
In this imperial power to the North, who have
Signed a pledge to engage in massive civil disobedience
If the U.S. military invades Nicaragua
As there are many signs they will—I too pray

On this Sunday morning in that infamous year of 1984
That the people of the world, before it is too late
Rise up like a gigantic dragon with the mightiest of roars
Rise up to end all wars
To find whatever wise and willing ways it takes
To make of atomic weapons and nuclear war
Only a nightmare and nothing more
To distribute fairly all around the globe
The wheat and other food now stored
In gigantic silos—kept away from the
Mouths of children in Ethiopia
Who can hardly move their jaws and teeth
Who have to be held, like wounded birds,
Turning their necks up, straining, crying out
For the tiniest morsel of bread, the smallest sip of soup

While in the industrial colossus
Of North America
The consumption
Of meat, the share of
Available protein,
And the incredible
Amount of waste
Must sometimes sicken
Anyone who
Values human life.
Sure the church
May gather contributions
For the poor
And other charities provide
Some small measure of relief
But they can never
In this way or by themselves
Stem the tide of tragedy
On this Sunday morning
In the mortuary where I live
It has become abundantly clear
That until the vast majority of us
Each one of us resolves
To take the smallest step
Along the road to peace and plenty
We will never know for sure

Another dawn, another child,
Another butterfly, another fawn.
Having to live with so much fear and doubt
The children wondering whether or not
Their lives will be lived out

Until the time
The human race
Acts for itself
Affirms its
Right to life
Our world
And deep
Inside our minds
Are destined to be
Torn by strife
No one has all the answers
I cannot tell you what to do
The Sun, just minutes ago so bright,
Is now almost completely hidden
Behind the clouds of war
Yet here and there
In struggling openings
The light comes shining through

The day, though stormy
Has come into its own
And so I end this Sunday morning poem
In this mortuary I now call my home.

Labor Pains of a Witch

The labor pains
Begin again
The hip still hurts
I think of trying
To bring the energy
Down to the ground
The labor pains
As I read *The First Sex*
And learn a Herstory
I never knew before
Worship of the Goddess
And of the goddess in
Each one of us — the
World of the craft,
The witch and the coven
Thirteen members
And if I were to have
A coven who would be
The people who would gather?
Chanting the spiral life force
Birth, death, and rebirth
Who would be the people
Who would gather?

Ode to the Octopus

Here come my tears
To greet the salt sea wind
Drip down my face
Filling up my ears
Run in rivulets
Down my body,
Over my shoulders,
My chest and stomach,
My hips and genitals,
Along my legs and feet,
Gushing out between my toes
On to the earth
Flowing in rivers
Like molten lava
To the ocean
Merging with
Eternal suffering
Swept out to sea
There to inebriate
With wine of human sadness
A wise old octopus
Who spits it out in ink
To write his eight-legged poetry.

Note: A well-known early internal Party essay by Mao Tse-tung criticizes what he called the "eight-legged essay" by which he meant one that rambles all over the place, goes in different directions, failing to come right out and say what it means—what we mean when we say "beating around the bush." The poem, however, is mainly about feeling sad.

Black Orchid

Black Orchid
Once open to the dawn
Now enslaved upon
The auction block
Of tears and tyranny
Beautiful flower
Bought and sold
In greed for gold
Delicate petals
Held in chain
Bid upon by leering men
What searing tragedy
What agonizing pain
Black Orchid
Enslaved upon
The auction block
Denied her liberty—
Yet only she
Can set her free:

Will bondage be her final doom
Or will she struggle into bloom?

Best Left Unsaid

This poem
Is dedicated to
The many things
In this world
Best left unsaid
And because
These things
Really are
Best left unsaid
And this poem
Is dedicated to them
Then this poem,
Although it may be read—
Is better left unsaid.

A Labor of Love

"In a labor of love, there is no labor."

There's magic
such strong power
In the ways
you turn a phrase
Seductively
to say the least

To say the most
May I toast
Your wise and loving
healing feeling
Heart and Art

Lord knows it's true
a labor of love
Does not spring forth
from that labor
We are forced to sell
So far below our human worth
in fields and factories
Fishmarkets, glass menageries
of this exploited earth

Yet and still
If you will
A labor of love
Can only come to birth
Through labor
Far more arduous
Than any other known

So funny valentine
When push comes to shove
Before more time has flown
Around the river bend
May I amend
As gently as I can
Your words above?

"In a labor of love
The labor is love."

A Strange Bloke

This is the story
Of a very strange gent
Who was never sure whether
He came or he went
One day he was happy
Next day he was sad
The law of the jungle:
To have or be had,
One day he was paid
Next day he was broke
This is the story
Of a kind-hearted bloke,
Who, trapped in obscurity,
Stymied by fate,
Nonetheless must be counted
As in his way great.

My Shortest Poem

My dear friend Bryan Nichols reminded me, when I sent
him a very short poem about George Bush, that I had once
written one even shorter. It was derived from a news
item on the continuing trail of bloodshed in the Middle
East—the assassination of Egyptian President Anwar
Sadat. The poem:

Sadat
Got
Shot.

The Bush poem is more recent and much longer:

Who Else But Bush

Don't blame it on the animals
They're not the source of sleaze
Who else but Bush could be the cause
Of foot-in-mouth disease?

Pharoah Sanders at S.F. State

Pharoah Sanders at San Francisco State
In the Student Union
My sister got free tickets
So, although it was sudden,
I decided to go, and am I glad I did
Because it was a spiritual experience
It was Rosh Hashanah eve, the New Year
Began to the incredibly beautiful
Saxophone of this great genius
Who looked out upon the audience
With dignity and grace, as he
Circular-breathed his way into my heart
The three other musicians
Also great and incredible—
A bassist who played like I've never seen
A drummer whose solid beat
And smiling face kept the spirit strong
And a piano player, understated but sometimes
On such flights of fantasy that I
Somehow mistook the music for a flute
And the great Pharoah, looking Egyptian
Eternal as the Sphinx, with a white wispy beard
Like Ho Chi Minh, playing his own
The Creator Has A Master Plan—having
A great time with the late 50s popular tune
"Too Young To Go Steady"—and in general
Inspiring me and many others with a
Special serenity and joy, a feeling of love, of
What it can mean to be human, of what
Beauty and artistry people can attain
No words, only music, can explain.

As I watched a tall woman in front of me
Weave in rhythm to the music, as I too
Vibrated deep inside, shook in sympathy
With the magic melodies and thrilling chords
Imbued with sentiment so heavenly
Infused with sensuality

And through it all the Pharoah looking out
Upon the people with a serious beneficence
Such a breathtaking ambiance
Long past the stage of technical facility
Playing the story of all humanity
No slavemaster Pharoah he—instead
A liberating force denouncing every slavery
And opening out into images of freedom wed
To landscapes of natural beauty and
The sound of seashells, the ringing of bells,
The thunder and roar of pacific oceans
Upon the shore of tenderest emotions
Amidst such thankful prayers and devotions
There and then I knew
That this New Year would bring
At last a time to help my spirit sing
When I would learn, in my own artistry
Circular breathing to sustain, maintain
The note of truth and beauty
To its natural, eventual conclusion

When all the terrors, traumas of the past,
Would come together, in a fusion
Of experience to celebrate the joy of life
Practice and passion overcoming strife
And I marvelled that here, amidst
The steel and concrete of the city
The screaming brakes, the violence
The cruelty, the rape, the sheer idiocy,
Could nevertheless arise this
Universal music of the spheres
Titled Black Classical Music on the poster
And so it is, and thus becomes
As one with all the greatest offerings
Of human beings to their existence
What a testament to the human spirit
That this exalted music could arise
From oppression and despair
That these magnificent waves of sound
Could fill the air, so otherwise polluted by
Industrial greed, that these courageous
Chords, these disciplined musicians, could
Amplify, with their souls and instruments
Such images of peace and harmony

Yes, truly, it was a sacred gathering for me
And when the Pharoah, who is also Moses,
Who is also Malcolm X and Martin Luther King
And every streetcorner blues musician
Whose genius has been reviled and ridiculed
By slavemasters of every cruel stripe

When the Pharoah sang, in his inimitable
Chanting, world-embracing, universal way,
Then played a high note, it seemed forever,
Then let the horn play by itself, then it seemed
As if the human blended with the note
The closest I have ever seen this unity
Once described in another's poetry
Who asked: how can we tell the dancer
From the dance? So I treasure this chance
I had to see this seer, this pure and fiery
Soul of prophecy, this divine and earthly artistry
Treasure the pleasure that I feel
In knowing that this at least is real
That on this spinning Mother Earth
These artists, like myself, brought to birth
Amidst the nuclear nightmare of
Our waking, quaking days
Have found within themselves a way
To give expression to the best in all of us
And I am honored, fortunate this day
To join their sacred meditation
To share their joyous celebration
From this moment on I walk out
Upon this Earth a better person
For having been a part of this
Blessed with a certain inner peace
Passed on by these high priests

From this day on, as New Year dawns,
I feel more natural, more able to
Perform my part, to start,
To open up my heart
To create each note, each day, anew
To make of life a work of art!!!!!!!!

What more can I say?
It was absolutely great—
Hearing Pharoah Sanders play
At San Francisco State!

Of Human Imperfection (All I Ask)
For Toby Garten   April 1985

On a throne of cement, rounded in an arc,
With stone mosaic inlays, green and white,
Depicting plants and animals, I sit alone
Beside the San Francisco Bay, looking out to
Alcatraz, lighthouse lamp circling inexorably
As the days and years and centuries
Served by prisoners within its walls
The famous Birdman, as well as Morton Sobell,
Whose crime was friendship with the Rosenbergs,
The lighthouse lamp circles in afternoon light,
Bright flowers bloom defiant purple on
The island's eastern shore, just as Indian peoples
Gathered in unity upon this same historic rock.

Beside me on the left, docked at adjoining pier
Looms World War II ship of war, the Jeremiah O'Brien
A "Liberty Ship" with daily tours from 9 to 4,
The wind is cool, the sunlight filters through
Light clouds, a few sailboats glide along,
The seagulls soar and whirl and ride the wind.

Across in the distance the shoreline of Marin
To the east, green and growing Berkeley/Oakland hills
Just to my right rugged coastline boulder
A lonely pine, bushy trees hug hillsides
Like seasoned lovers who know each other well
Yet cling excitedly as gusts of passion
Sculpt and mold their branches and their leaves
Vegetation green and golden brown, thick as pubic hair,
A California poppy here and there, as sitting on my throne
I see a scrawled graffiti near my feet: "FUCK ME"
Look up atop the battleship, on the foredeck
A painted cartoon drawing of a woman with
Large naked breasts and "G" string
"Miss Jerry O'Brien," scrawled on grey metal wall;
Slim cannon set at angle of erection,
Its silhouette sceptered against the sky.

Here I am, at 40, would-be-writer, sitting on my throne.
At long last happier, better sense of solitude,
Learning how to love and live alone.
As warclouds threaten out of Washington,
I set here peacefully, near Fort Mason
Military bastion now blessedly become

A cultural mecca in this city of St. Francis,
Sword transformed into ploughshares
Cornucopia of non-profit organizations
Environmental, arts, and theatre groups
And in one of these offices sits a woman
It has been my joy to come to know
Looking through manila folders of job listings
Ceaseless need to earn one's livelihood.

A tugboat passes, churning white foam
Tourist helicopter circles overhead
Wind seems to be subsiding just a bit
More warmth of sun gets through to me—
"Give me a subject," I implored, before
I left to sit upon this throne and write
And she, whose mind can be like mercury,
Quick and silvery, elusive as a Pisces,
Replied, "How about human imperfection?"
We'd read a passage on the subject earlier
And she and I agreed that this is precisely
What makes people interesting,
Makes humans human, connects us all
To one another, each to each,
Off in the distance, seagulls shriek
Wind rises once again, air colder now,
Waves improvise new cadence on the shore
Eddy round the log beam pillars of the pier
Baby seagull floats serene on dappled waves.

Spirit of the sea, of sun and sky and wind
Bless this moment with infinite tenderness
Of motherhood, manatee with infant to her breast,
Give us the wisdom and the strength
To return to nature what she gives to us, to evolve—
Precisely through our imperfections—
Into a species for whom war is nothing more
Than a vestigial organ of the body politic.

I wish the human race
And every human face
Could be as seagull circling free—
Imperfect world it still would be
Illness, conflict, jealousy,
Yet wonderful as it could get
If only one condition were met:
All I ask, as this great bay,
Beats loving heart upon the shore
Is for a world with no more war.

Beginnings and Endings: for Efrem

Beginnings and Endings
The Acupuncturist
Told me how Chinese medicine
Connects the Grief emotion
To the intestines
As he treated me
For a painful
Somewhat mysterious malady...

Beginnings and Endings
Separations
How to say goodbye
Holding the sadness in,
Or as he said once before
Some Deep Holding
Holding in the grieving
For a long time — yes said I
At least 21 years
Since my mother's death
And also Elsa, and he said
The recent separation
Yes I agreed, and he said
Beginnings and Endings
That's really all he needed
To say that day
Because with his treatment
I cried and cried
My body shaking, quaking,
Tears filling up my ears
The needles sticking out all over me

How to say goodbye
It has its parallels in writing
In all of creativity

Beginnings and Endings
Letting the energy flow in a circle
Not worrying
Not holding the energy inside

Today was a healing feeling experience
Some part of what is trapped inside
Could no longer be repressed, denied,
Had to be expressed, so may
My future life be blessed
With an ability to calmly flow
To let it go...to tell it on the mountain
To tell my story
In all of its intricate
Weavings and blendings
In the words of the acupuncturist:
Beginnings and Endings...

January 1985

Note: This poem was published in the excellent book on Chinese and Western medicine entitled *Between Heaven and Earth*, written by Efrem Korngold and Harriet Beinfield, who practice healing arts at Chinese Medicine Works in San Francisco.

There is a time....

there is a time when
the tide
takes over
rolling unstoppable
to the tune of
its mistress the moon
a time when love
and death and taxes
are subsumed in
waves of passion
wonderful and wild
such a time
is the conception
and birth
of a child

I Will Always Remember You Singing
for Dick Broadhead

Can it be true
What they said—
My old friend
Dick Broadhead dead?

If I had wings like Noah's dove
I'd fly cross the river
To the one I love
Fare thee well my honey
Fare thee well...

I remember him singing
The clear high voice ringing
The beautiful sincerity
The shining smiling eyes
I remember him singing

The water is wide
I cannot cross o'er
Neither have I wings to fly
Give me a boat
That can carry two
And both shall row
My love and I

I remember him singing
Freedom songs on picket lines
Gonna let that little light shine
For a time, we were closest friends,
I can't believe how soon it ends
Memories of early years
Tears and triumphs,
Dreams and fears,
Surge of struggle, joy of love
If I had wings like Noah's dove...

Sad to say in recent times
I did not know him well
Still I hope my humble rhymes
Communicate that special spirit
In his singing I can hear it
You see, I knew him way back when
So I knew in some small fashion
Fertile soil from whence he grew
His tenderness, compassion, sharing
Leadership of strength and caring
The laughter and the energy
Of working hard collectively
I knew him when
Deep singing Springs
Of his sweet giving soul
Turned into a river's flow
So that is how I also know:
His living spirit helps us grow.

If I had wings like Noah's dove
I'd fly cross the river
To the one I love
Fare thee well, my honey, fare thee well...

Dick, I will always remember you singing...

Note: Richard "Dick" Broadhead was a very close friend of mine at Deep Springs College. He became an outstanding math teacher and union leader at Berkeley High. He died tragically, way too young, of a very aggressive cancer. This poem was recited at a memorial for him in Berkeley.

Land of Lakes

Long ago in that now faraway lost land of lakes
Screen doors were used to keep mosquitoes out.
And when I came, dripping after a swim,
Running over the grass, past the garden where
I found agates and didn't eat the toadstools,
I'd push through the door into the warm house,
Run up the winding stairs and dry myself.
But that was long ago, and in the land of lakes.

Once, after running over the grass, I pushed
At the screen door and it didn't move. Someone
Had locked it from the inside. Always after,
Just in case, I approached the screen door with
Caution, remembering the time it sent
Sharp jolt all up my arm when it was locked.

And that was long ago, and in my childhood land
Where once when I fell off the dock, not knowing
How to swim I curled up like a fetus on
The bottom of the lake. And I guess I would have
Drowned had not my father rescued me. Drowned—
Then never walked down dusty dirt roads, in
Search of carnelians, lustrous red agates with intricate layers,
Created in the changes of the geologic ages.

My ages also passed, and only locked forever
Memories remain with me. For my life among the lakes
Lies buried like I was in water, and the memories
Surface like my breathy bubbles did. Even those
Illusions have been burst by now, like cherished
Childhood teddy bear torn to pieces by a lonely dog.

Death like an older boy, laughing as he pops the bubbles
Little children blow, smashing the warped TV screen
Reflections of the world. And I am gone from that land, now
Stretched before the TV watching "Route 66,"
(How different from those dusty roads I walked for agates.)
The show's about an orphan's anguished search for a mother
He never finds, and tears come to my eyes.
Next to me lies a falsely pregnant dog nursing a stuffed rabbit,
As on TV, they speed down the asphalt,
Through the torn cities, meeting people, stopping
At houses where I would be only a responsible stranger.
Solemn soul searching for warmth again, looking at the
Begging jobless men, looking into other lonely eyes.

In that lonely land of lakes, before I learned to swim
I wore my swimming trunks to bed where I'd pretend
To be doing an expert crawl before I went to sleep.
Was I embarrassed when my babysitter felt them
Underneath the covers! I pretended to be asleep—
How much I yearned to swim!

Now, I watch world writhe with violent racism, see
Hate and indifference wrestle with a working
Sisterbrotherhood, stare into scared and
Cynical teenage eyes, yet also meet other eyes
Whose minds are stayed on freedom, on that prize,
I feel a fearful combat in my heart and mind
Miss that certain look, unable to fully join in,
Can't seem to reach out and take offered hand
Watching, not riding, the waves of our land.

And that was long ago, and in my childhood land of lakes
Blessings of extended family rang out
Like hootenanny "hammer song" and "Union Maid"
Gatherings of "progressive" kids at Meridel's
Grandpa in Shriner hat takes us to the circus
Picnic at Como Park or Minnehaha Falls
Mississippi River houseboats still wind through my dreams
I was so impressed when I briefly met
A girl my age who lived on a houseboat
Ah, six-years-old and call it love!
I treasure carnelians with every layer of my being
I pray that I may yet have what it takes
To open up my memories until at last and once again I find
That long ago, no longer lost, lost land of lakes.

Note: This poem evoking my early childhood in Minnesota
was mostly written sometime in the early and mid-sixties,
with an early version sent to my grandparents. I'm not sure
that the version I sent reflected as much existential angst as
this one—interesting to wonder what they perceived from it.
There is something haunting about this poem for me. I have
come back to it again and again and never quite able to "get
it right." This is another attempt. The last stanza was
written upon reflection after many years—I added it in 1995.

Collective Poem #1   Childhood Memories

February 2, 1983
Home for Jewish Parents
Free Expression/Poetry Class

I remember
I remember
Far far back I remember:

> I remember
> My grandparents
> We lived a few blocks away
> My sister and I
> When we were five and six
> Would sometimes
> Go over to their house
> For breakfast
> And they wouldn't start eating
> Until we got there
> They were so happy to see us
> They could hardly wait
> They wanted us to
> Sit on their laps
> They could hardly wait
> Until we got there
> So happy to see us
> So impatient, so eager
> For us to get there
> And climb upon their laps
> Yes, I remember
> Those happy breakfasts
> With my grandparents
> They loved us so much
> So happy to see us
> Could hardly wait
> Until we got there...

I remember
I remember
Far far back I remember:

I remember
When I was only two years old
My parents left me
With an aunt
They were going to a wedding
And I was not allowed to go
I remember how I cried
I cried and cried, inconsolable
Until she said to me,
"If you stop crying
I will give you
A brand new dress."
And right then and there
She brought it out
I remember it so well
A beautiful beautiful dress
With tiny black polka dots
All over it—I'll never forget
That beautiful dress
Right then and there
I stopped crying—only
Two years old, yet still
I remember that beautiful dress.

I remember
I remember
Far far back
Yet still I remember:

I remember one Yom Kippur
I was twelve years old
My parents were away all day
And all day long
I fasted, all day long,
When my parents returned
I told them what I'd done
They were happy, they smiled
At how seriously
I'd taken the Day of Atonement
Yes, I remember
When I was twelve years old
I fasted all day long.

I remember
I remember
Far far back I still remember
Not only happiness
That I remember:

> For I remember
> At first our life
> It was all right
> There was a big synagogue
> And we were able to get by
> Until the pogroms,
> The Cossacks, the war,
> The Polish soldiers
> Then the memories
> Turn sad, turn violent
> My childhood shattered
> By fear and persecution
> At first it was all right
> But then the terror came

I remember
I remember
The nightmare terror
Of our lives:

> I remember
> When I was
> A young girl in Vienna
> I remember the food parcels
> Coming from the United States
> And I remember
> Hitler's rise to power
> And how we had to escape
> Going to Shanghai China
> Hitler's rise to power
> The nightmare terror
> Of our lives

164

I remember
I remember
All of this I must remember

And yet
Within that inward eye
Despite the hardship
Still survives
A sense of human dignity
A love of natural beauty:

       I remember
       I remember
       I've been 72 years here
       But still I remember
       I can never forget
       In Russia when I was a child
       We lived in a small town—
       Across from our house
       Fields stretched for miles
       Fields of wheat
       And what I remember most of all
       Was how, in February, in the winter,
       When snow covered everything
       And the snow was dirty
       Beginning to melt
       As the very first signs of spring began
       I will always remember
       Can never ever forget
       How the fresh bright green
       Of newly growing wheat
       Rose up against the snow
       I will never get over it
       Never anything so beautiful
       So beautiful, so beautiful
       Never anything so beautiful!

Yes, we remember, we remember
From generation to generation
We remember:

I remember when
>My grandson
>Said his first complete sentence—
>Standing up in bed
>My grandson said:
>"Mommy, can you hear the birds singing?"

Yes, we can hear
The birds of poetry singing
As we remember
The fresh green wheat of spring
Against the snow
As we reflect upon
The joys and terrors of our lives
We remember
We can still remember
And as we speak
We become poets
We become the birds singing
Yes, gathered here in Oakland
As winter changes into spring
We can hear the birds of beauty sing!

Note: This poem received an award from the Western Gerontological Society. It is a collage of the memories of some of the 20 people for whom I was honored to present a weekly class during the time my father resided in this Oakland facility.

For Elsa with Love

The first time
I ever heard
Your voice
I listened and I learned
And a great wheel
Within me turned
And later
When we worked together
In troubled times
Through stormy weather
Our voices joined
So clear and strong
To sing resistance song

Yes, Elsa we have always shared
A tender love of truth
A sense of reaching out respectfully
A deep and very very special
Spiritual communication
A passionate determination
And all of this we'll always share
No matter where our bodies may reside

Because
When I am
At the microphone
You are always
At my side
Whether it is
You or I who
Say the words
It is the same
Life force
Transmitting through us
That spreads
Its energies far and wide

In this our quest
To heal the human soul
Through true communication
You have been my greatest teacher
Neither false prophet nor pie-sky preacher
Instead, a forerunner, a revolutionary
Always alive to what is new
A firm but loving guide to what is true

And as you have been to me
So have you been to
So many others
Who have gone on to share
The vision of a world
Where sisters and brothers
Plant the flowers of the future

Dearest Elsa
The power of your artistry
The meaning of your work and life
Rising, as it had to,
Over so much pain and strife
Has given us a legacy
Beyond my powers to describe
As even now
Your words echo so melodically
In voices all around the earth
In the cry of every child
Who meets the light of birth

Yes, your legacy
Is as you wished it
It is fruitful, it multiplies,
The echoes of
Your ceaseless years
Of full-throated song
Entwine so deep within
Each winding root of life revived.

Your principles and your belief
Spread out like veins upon a leaf
Hearing you, the bud
Aches at last to open
Feels sure the blossoming will come
Despite the warclouds
Threatening from above
Yet shall burst forth
Beautiful flowers of your love

Flowers of justice and freedom
Surge on every shore
Triumphant like your spirit
Over need, and greed, and war

And should you die
The only thing
For all of us to do
Is to let your spirit
Help us through
By always
Staying tuned to you.

Note: Elsa Knight Thompson, as mentioned in the Acknowledgments, passed on many lessons to me. While a number of outstanding journalists have passed through KPFA's portals, it was Elsa, as Public Affairs Director for many years, who established the lasting reputation of the station for incisive interviews, defense of freedom of speech, compassion, justice, and truth. Her interviews are legendary, including those with Paul Robeson and James Baldwin, Ella Winter, Huey Newton and Bobby Seale, and hundreds of others, many of them famous but others like the ordinary GI disenchanted with Vietnam. Elsa did not suffer fools gladly; she had a sharp tongue, unwavering principles, and what Hemingway called a "built-in shock-proof shit detector." She had made it in a man's world, been a leading broadcaster at the BBC during and after World War II, and brought deep political commitment and journalistic integrity to KPFA and Pacifica. Her career there was stormy. Fired for political reasons, a strike ensued at the station and she won her job back. Many years later, she was forcibly retired by a crew of crass opportunists who almost destroyed the station, and damn near broke her heart. Still later she received the first Lewis Hill Award for distinguished service to Pacifica, but it was too little too late. Elsa always said that the "whole is greater than the sum of its parts" and she supported the KPFA-Pacifica democratic experiment regardless of her own fate within it, but I must add that KPFA and Pacifica have failed to understand how to use more experienced elders to pass on lessons to new programmers. They also have, against her better judgment, accepted government funds, and, though they espouse democracy, have failed to implement democratic principles in their own organization. As Elsa once put it, "an organization cannot claim to tell the truth about the world and fail to tell the truth about itself." Elsa was, to those who knew her well, a responsive, honest, loyal, and consistent friend, a wise and compassionate soul, whose acid wit often hoisted the rightwing and its sycophants on their own petard.

Love Sky for Lisa

I. Love Sky

This is true:
The sky of night
Turned blue
The sun took
One more encore
Harbor waves
Caressed the shore
Strong and longingly
Passion aching to be born
In each other's eyes
We were a lovely sight
The sky we could have sworn
Was dark as night
Dawned anew in dream of bliss
We lit the darkness with our kiss

II. Oh, What A Night

Rare indeed, those moments when
Two people find such joy and solace
In knowledge of each other, the finest wine,
The most expensive caviar,
The fastest car, even a perfect pear,
Cannot compare to those magic moments
Seemingly standing still in time
Yet so full of wave and motion
In a poetry of ocean
Something to savor forever
    Never will the smell, the taste, the feeling fade
    Oh, what a night, oh what a love we made.

III.

At last the mortuary
Has been consecrated
The press of flesh
The lick of kiss
The hold of hug
At last the cemetery
Of my aching soul
Bursts into summer bloom
Transforms, becomes reborn
O sweet Lord above
Now I know the only
Sacrament is Love.

IV.

Our shy yet so amazing grace
At last has found
Its time and place.

Oyster Ecstasy

Dearest could you ever know
All the ways I love you so?
Though the bitter winds do blow
You give me shelter from the snow
Nestled in your tenderness
I sense again true happiness
Yes as we cling closer still
I know that come what may we will
Cherish with our gentle hearts
Music, rhyme, and all the arts
For in your shining eyes I see
The oyster of our ecstasy
Whatever winds the new years bring
A song of love to you I sing.

The Land of What If

In the land of What If
Where I travel sometimes
You just start to talk
And like magic it rhymes

In the land of What If
Where the wishberries bloom
If Love is the yarn
Life is the Loom

Weaving colorful carpets
To fly on with friends
To soar to the place
Where the Child never ends

So come with me folks
Don't be stuffy or stiff
Laugh, love, and be loose
In the Land of What If.

Ecstasy   3/23/86

Ecstasy perches
High on a cliff of Kauai
Here, near the lighthouse,
Ecstasy begins to rise
A magic rainbow-colored
Bird from Paradise...

Ecstasy glides
In and out, over and under
Sun and clouds play tag
Arching dolphins
Dance and somersault below
To rhythms of the sea
In their own ecstatic glee...

The champagne cork
Ascends to the heavens
Conversations and emotions
Outpouring naturally
The children blossoming
Like purple orchids
Wind conversing with the leaves...

The sun beats heat upon the land
The ocean breathes
It is so breathtakingly beautiful
Here, where Ecstasy perches
Upon a cliff, near the lighthouse,
The strong and gentle horses graze—
Ah, truly halcyon days!

Here, where Ecstasy
Spreads wings
To soar above
With power of Love
To celebrate
With reverence
And laughter
How good life is...

Each of us carrying
Our own intricate personalities
Family histories, secrets and intrigues,
Ways of being alone and with others—
To each of us there is a season
A time for every purpose
As with the waving trees
The hibiscus and the bees
No rhyme without reason —
To everything there is a season...

The world is charged
With the grandeur of Love
Ecstasy, the magic bird,
Flies high above, then
Returns, enfolds us in warm wings,
Embracing all of us, till
Smiles, and eyes, and faces all express
The radiance of Happiness!

To Deborah and the Goddess of the Clay

from Lincoln with Love, August, 1986

Elements of energies
Energies of elements
Combine and recombine
Some scholars say
That hidden in the
Heart of clay
May be the way
To comprehend the mystery
Of how all life first came to be...

Well, as for me
Up here in Sonoma
Near the vast Pacific
In Graton, to be more specific
I have seen living proof
Of all this theoretical speculation
So I present this declaration
On this great day of celebration:

Yes, verily, with my own eyes
I've seen the living spirit rise
In birthing plates
And fountain goddesses
Whose bodies ripen like pears
I've seen the clay infused
With spark of light and life
Glow in a glaze ablaze
With love and growth and change
From lump of earth
I've seen this clay
Brought into birth
By one whose hands and body
Center on the wheel of creation
Turning and turning
Yearning and learning
With sweat and blood and inspiration

Yes, and I have watched amazed
Her quest so constant for the glaze
Not some commercial treasure-hunt
For perfect hues or shades
Not journey for some Holy Grail
Though the search is very sacred

More like a circle, ever-widening
Not to succeed or fail
Not to win or lose in some
Linear abstract ambition
But to approach and gather in
With all-embracing intuition.

Each glaze to fit the molded shape
As pea to pod or skin to grape
Each to pursue its own direction
Cast its own unique reflection
Shine its special pigmentation
Share its essence of creation

All held and brought together
In work of lasting human worth
Grown like a flower from the earth
It is here, near the Pacific
In Graton, to be more specific
Where I see, from
Deborah's heart and art
The clay come leaping into birth!

Even as she
A relatively few years ago
Sprang into being
Grew into the person we are seeing
Who brings creation to the clay
The play of work, the work of play
One of the reasons
We are gathered here today
Is to wish a Happy Earth Birthday
Or we might also say
Singing sweet and true
Happy Birth Clay to You!

Caitlin's Birth Announcement

Pound the gong and beat the drum
A child into this world has come
Sound shofar and strum guitar
Let music echo near and far
Hug the harp and kiss the horn
For the babe who's just been born
Clap your hands and ring the bell
Caitlin's born and all is well !!!!!

The Toucan Do Song

Can you do what the toucan do?
I can do what the toucan do
Toucan can play peek-a-boo
I can play peek-a-boo too…

Can you do what the toucan do?
I can do what the toucan do
The can-can dance in a new tutu
I can do the can-can too…

Can you do what the toucan do?
I can do what the toucan do
Toot a tune on her blue kazoo
I too toot on my blue kazoo…

Can you do what the toucan do?
I can do what the toucan do
Hop around like a kangaroo
I can hop like a kanga too…

Two can do what the toucan do
You can do what the toucan do
One can't do what two can do, but
We all can do what the toucan do!

177

A Child's First Christmas in Berkeley

Waking in her mother's arms
The colors, shapes, and sounds
Shift in kaleidoscopic swirl
Around her, as from deep
Recesses of genetic consciousness
Her personality emerges from cocoon.

Who is this Caitlin Poema?
Awakened a few weeks early,
Already smiling at the foam rubber
Leaping lizard bouncing up and down,
Enamored of the smiling face shape
On the wall by the changing table—
Who is this Caitlin Poema?
Experiencing her first holiday season
The colored lights sparkle on the tree
At gatherings she is passed from
Arm to arm, sharing her magical newness,
The sweet smell of her hair
That perfect soft nuzzling place
At the nape of her tiny neck.

Father walking her, sister teaching,
Family and friends hugging and kissing
The mobile above her crib goes round
Earth spins upon Her axis
Winter comes in with silvery veils
And the little house in Berkeley
Is cold in temperature, but warm with Love.

Waking in her mother's arms
Caitlin Poema gives suck
Drinks in the nourishing nectar
The only true ambrosia
Her lips and mouth caress the nipple
Ecstatic meeting of the need to feed—
She looks up at Lisa with such
Eager, wise, and trusting eyes—
Within this child, as in all others,
Run rivers of remembered ancestors
The one-time-only coded collage
Spanning the first spark of life
In oozing tidepool countless moons ago
Reflecting all the animals, herself included,
Giving suck, like some small furry creature,
Waking in her mother's arms.
In deep sleep, so peaceful

Would that our world
Could be that way—

That Justice could rock the cradle
Of a world where
South African emancipation
Nicaraguan self-determination
Would symbolize the possibility
Of Peace for the entire Rainbow Race
Caitlin's tiny features shine
Such beautiful expressions
What child is this?
Who is this Caitlin Poems?
This sweet and lovely child—
Human infant, tender, mild.

Caitlin cries, is picked up in
Her father's arms, quiets down,
Looks all around, begins to
Push and strain, then pause
Then push and strain again
Until she gets it out
And needs to be changed
Then not long afterward
Her cry of hunger sounds a summons
She settles down to suck once more
Nestled in her mother's arms.

Christmas on Rose Street
The harp and horn
Stand gentle sentinel
Door-harp sends out
Bell-like tones that
Caitlin hears, with
Eyes wide and ears opening
Like wildflowers to the light.

A child's first Christmas in Berkeley
The colored lights, the family and friends,
The smell of cookies baking
Voices, music, and laughter
Blend in memories that ever after
Will be held in that unconscious
But somehow remembered place
Where lives the hidden pleasure
Of our first awakenings to the Spirit
Of Love and Happiness and Human Worth
That yet may inherit the Earth!

Selections from Redwood Rhapsodies

I. January 16th 1987

First words from a new house
On Milvia between Cedar and Vine
Across the street from me
A beautiful redwood tree
Hundreds of years old
Stands living witness
Beneath the full moon
Aglow above the Berkeley hills.

I sit with Caitlin on my lap
Anna is asleep on the couch
The moon is full upon the world
Fraught with contention.

It remains my intention
To write my poetry
But so far at least
It does not pay the rent.

I sit and look out —
So sang Walt Whitman
As he catalogued
The woes and sorrows
The human race visits
Upon itself—the redwood tree
Testifies in the full light of the moon.

II. January 19, 1987

The Klan breaks up a civil rights march
Commemorating Martin Luther King
In an all-white county down in Georgia—
Andrew Young predicts the
Racist regime of South Africa is bound to fall.

Day before yesterday
A neighborhood chase
Of an alleged purse-snatcher
Led to his arrest
In front of our house
A tall, strongly-muscled
Black man in his early twenties
Being held by a Black policeman
Leaning despondently but defiantly on
The police car being watched
By all the neighbors, mostly white.

Anna and I almost saw it begin
Several blocks away as the
Man hurtled by on the other side
Of the block with another man
In hot pursuit, shouting, "Stop Thief!!!"
And later Anna watched very intently
As the man stood abjectly
Then finally was hauled away.

The redwood tree watched too.

Redwood #4

A Sunday afternoon
The weather is warming
First signs of Spring
Beginning blossomings

Caitlin likes the sun
Likes to lie naked
Moving her arms and legs
All akimbo, as
Movement by movement
Frame by frame
Her mind and body
Get to know each other
Hand-eye coordination
Every instant an experiment.

She sleeps as
Lisa and I entwine.

Later thick bushy redwood leaves
Sway slightly in the cooling breeze
The clouds suggest rain
Sun sets on sleepy Sunday afternoon.

Later Redwood Interlude

Night skies have been especially clear
Orion's belt distinct and luminous above me
The redwood tree casts its nighttime shadow
Deep and dark from the crystalline light of the stars.

Redwood #6

Last Friday night, April 24
Was the occasion of
An hilarious exchange
Of uproarious laughter
Between Anna and Caitlin
Joined by Lisa and me
As Anna twirled around
In front of Caitlin
Then sang out shrilly —
"Peek-a-boo!"
And Caitlin laughed
And laughed and laughed
In utter glee and
The rest of us joined in
Laughing merrily —

Merrily, I say unto you
That it is moments like these
That need to be written down
Lest in more trying times
Our agonies outweigh our ecstasies
And we forget that life
Shines so brightly
In moments of laughter like these.

The redwood tree
No doubt understands that
Observing various families
Beneath her branches
The redwood tree is nurtured by
The strains of music
And laughter that send
Sweetly caressing soundwaves
Amidst all her branches
The same is true
For the other plants and trees
They all know that
Life shines so brightly
In moments of laughter like these.

In moments of laughter like these
In moments of laughter like these
Life shines so brightly
The dance turns to sprightly
In moments of laughter like these.

Redwood #12

We become
What we become,
Seemingly
By chance and choice,
But actually,
As inexorably
As ripening plum,
Or redwood tree.

So as you grow,
To live and love,
Be reminded of
One rule of thumb:
We become
What we become.

Rock of Wages

Rock of wages
Cleft for me
End this
Mindless misery

For I work hard
Every day
And I try to
Save my pay
But my bills
Are overdue
And my debts are
Rising too

Rock of wages
Cleft for me
Let me win
The Lottery!

Yom Kippur 1988

Yom Kippur
I hear, I fear
My father's health is failing.
Yom Kippur
I ask
How long O Lord
Before the mournful wailing?
How long before
This passionate saga
Of labor and love
Runs its rocky course
Into a sea of death?

Is death
As many believe
Merely passageway
To another stage?

If so, then why do
The strongest strugglers
Among us rage so against it
Their every blood vessel
Surging with the words
Of Dickens— "life is
Given to us on the
Definite understanding
That we defend it to the last."

There are no answers,
Only questions, only seekers,
And yet the power of prayer
Offers solace even to those of us
Who find organized religion
Unequal to the spiritual tasks
We face along the pilgrimage of life.

For what is a prayer
If not a poem?

My father was a poet
And I'm a poet's son
And I'll keep making poems
Until my life is done.

Preparing for My Father's Death

Dear Pa
Now just a shadow
Of your former self
Still your vigor and vitality
Will live in us always
Your humor in adversity
All your special qualities
Sometimes so stubborn
With your share of error and terror
But always Pa and especially for you today
I take this solemn vow...
For you Beloved Comrade
The fight will still go on
The fight will still go on...
And when
Your body can
No longer rise
To see another dawn
When you are gone

I will remember you
Return
Within my heart and mind
To treasure all the times
When your
Dynamic spark
Lit up the dark
The conversations
The joyous arguments
The struggle and the art
All play their part
Upon this stage
The deeds and words
They do not die
They still are heard—

The passover
From one generation to the next
Contains the lessons of the past
Helps nurture and sustain
The striving for a time at last
When oppression and injustice cease
And people live in dignity and peace.

How to prepare
For the inevitable
How to prepare
For all the emotional trauma
Raised as you reach
The closing chapter of your days?

Dear Pa
The poet Pa
Before your final
Lines are writ
I want to make it clear
That we shall carry
What death can never bury

I want these lines to show
Want you to know
That your vast grasp
Extends far beyond
Your final gasp
Much farther
Than we can ever know
They say
The child is parent
To the person grown
I say too the
Child within us never dies
And is constantly reborn
In all of those
We've somehow helped
To make it through
Comrades lovers and friends
The road never ends.

Dear Pa
In my life
I will do
What I have to do
As did you
With as much
Clarity and courage
As I can muster

Death comes to all
On this off-center ball
But through it all
I will always recall
So many of your words and deeds
Your death will hit me hard
I know, yet even now, within me,
I can feel strength grow
To let emotions flow
To let emotions flow
When final push meets final shove
All I feel for you
Is LOVE!

Love Sonnet to My Father After His Death

When I envision you I see a flame
A comet flash across a starry sky
Rebellion must have been your middle name
I loved the leap of laughter in your eye.
Dear Pa, your spirit lives on like a poem
Whose meaning only deepens over time
As over years our friendship too has grown
We share a lifelong love affair with rhyme.
There are no words to tell you how I feel
The grieving sinks like stone into my heart
Great legacy of struggle is so real
Your joy in living, energy, and art.
These lines are writ as well as I am able
With all my deepest love to Papa Leibel.

For My Father   May 5, 1989

Your birthday today
Six months have passed
Since you were laid to rest
In consecrated earth

Well, either he's buried in
Consecrated earth, or he's not...
And if he is, well,
What's there to worry about?

So went the saw
You used to tell
About the Russian rabbi...

At any rate
You'd be amazed
Chinese students have erupted recently
Just in time for May 4th
The Palestinian Intifada
Has awakened the Middle East
Abbie Hoffman met his maker...

Your daughter and sons survive
And even thrive
Your granddaughters growing
Like wildflowers of Freedom and Spring.

We had a nice Seder
It wasn't the same without you
And had dinner with your brother the rabbi
Just last night—also heard
Your old comrade Will has
Taken a turn for the worse again
It's days and times like these when
I feel your loss the most, that emptiness,
Meanwhile, still endeavoring to pursue
My own happiness, I end this poem
And think of you.

For Abbie Hoffman (as broadcast)

After a few weeks reflection, I am still only just beginning to fully realize what a deep and tragic loss has taken place. I believe it is well-nigh impossible to overestimate the psychological impact that the early death of Abbie Hoffman is having on my psyche and millions of others of my times and generation. The coroner's finding of suicide and the revelations concerning manic depression somehow only serve to make his tremendous resilience and political acumen over the years all the more remarkable.

Abbie Hoffman. I didn't know him well, met him a few times. We shared a number of close friends, so I heard of him over the years. I interviewed him back in 1972, along with longtime activist Stew Albert, and what, if memory serves, was quite a cast of characters lounging around the larger KPFA studio. Freedom Is A Constant Struggle is going to play that interview for you in a few minutes.

Abbie was a real rebel to the core, the revolutionary impulse and irreverent humor blending in a unique individual, whose sheer daring and chutzpah were only exceeded by his commitment and dedication to social change. I especially thrill to his creation of an underground self, Barry Freed, who became a well-known environmental activist, even appointed to a Presidential commission, testifying before a Congressional committee, and photographed with New York Senator Moynihan. I also remember what I know of the vast spectrum of Abbie's political experience, from the demonstrations against the House Un-American Activities Committee in San Francisco as the 60s dawned through the South during the civil rights movement, the movement against the war in Vietnam, the student movement, youth culture, the Chicago conspiracy trial—the momentous demonstrations crushed by the FBI and the jackboots of Mayor Daley senior's Chicago storm troopers, the Youth International Party, or YIPPIES, with Pig-a-sus the Pig running for President, the long years underground, the environmental activism, the demonstrations for Central American and South African freedom, the weapon of humor, the searing satires, the books with titles like *Steal this Book*, the sheer presence of this man, dressed in an American flag, arrested at least 42 times, well, nothing I can say could really do him justice, so:

Listen, Abbie Hoffman, wherever you may be
Listen to this poem from the heart of me:

On the same day
Sugar Ray Robinson and Abbie Hoffman

Sugar Ray
Suffering from Alzheimer's
Years of strife
The bittersweet of death and life
Yet Sugar Ray
Was dignity and grace
His choreography and courage
All the while
Spelled victory with style.

Same for Abbie
His humor and wit
Unflagging bravery
Brilliant irony
Inspiring and organizing
Compassion and commitment
Great comic smile
Spelled victory with style.

Boxing is brutal.
So is politics.

April 12, 1989
Will be remembered as the day
When two great fighters died.

Like Tom Paine, Abbie was a great citizen of the world.
Or as Allen Ginsberg said, "He was a great rebel, a
revolutionist, and one of the most honorable men of our
times." Moments that live on, as this country and the
world are poised on the brink of the 1990s, the final
decade of this century. Like John Brown, Abbie Hoffman
may be dead, but his soul goes marching on. Thank you
very much for listening and have a good night.

On Jerry Rubin's Death

November 29, 1994

Jerry Rubin dies
Two days before
Abbie Hoffman's birthday

Jerry dies after being hit by a car
Jaywalking across Wilshire Boulevard in L.A.
Or, as Lenin is said to have said:
While crossing alone over icebergs
As they crashed down around him
He trudged onward thinking:
"What a stupid way to die."

I see Jerry most of all
In Revolutionary War outfit
Before the House Un-American Activities Committee
Made front pages everywhere
Brilliant propaganda stroke
Finishing touches on that ignoble tool
Of the Anti-Communist inquisition...

So they say
In later years Rubin
Became an entrepreneur
Got into Wall Street, health food
Always did have plenty of public relations flair
But I prefer to remember him
With the other seven conspirators in Chicago
At Berkeley's Free Speech Movement
And helping lead the Vietnam Day Committee—
Who of us, I'm forced to ask,
Has proven equal to the task?

When Jerry, where spirits gather, meets Abbie
After whatever unfinished business they may have
Expect great sparks of yippie energy
Irrepressive as freedom's pulse
Individualized in the extreme
Yet committed to collective anarchy

Bursting at the seams with laughter
Wearing a Revolutionary war costume
Long hair, beard, love beads, incense,
Holding picket signs and banners,
Aloft in rainbows of diversity—
Can we my friends expect to see such times again
When we were all called "sisters" "brothers"
Took to the streets in "affinity groups"
When we looked out upon the world
With the eyes of justice-loving children, and
When a pig named Pigasus ran for President!

For John Belushi

Forget the reasons, just give the blues their due
Forget the reasons, just give the blues their due
When it came to comedy, his aim was all too true.

Smacked us on the funnybone, in mad demonic glee
Smacked us on the funnybone, in mad demonic glee
Cocaine blues for John Belushi, dead at thirty-three.

That 'bro was out there, stomped upon the stage
That 'bro was really out there, stompin' on the stage
Two parts wild and crazy, and one part solid rage.

So forget the reasons, but pay the blues some dues
Yeh, forget the reasons, and pay the blues some dues
Got to laugh to keep from crying, sing those John Belushi blues.

Red Rose for Huey Newton 1989

I.
I remember Huey
When his eyes were shining bright
I remember Huey
When his smile lit up the ghetto
With its fierce burning light
I remember Huey
When he spoke the truth so clear
He inspired in our captors
Reactionary fear
I remember Huey
When he wore a black beret
Chanting power to the people
Calling forth a better day.

Did he falter? Did he waver?
Did his demons do him in?
Surely Huey was no stranger
To slave wages we call sin.
Yet and still he was a leader
Many moments in the sun
On the patchwork quilt of freedom
We remember what he's done
Yet and still for all his failings
Weaknesses and fears
Yet and still he was a leader
Remembered through the years
We knew we needed leaders
Did we fancy they would be
Somehow superhuman
Or immune to frailty?

II.
Addiction is affliction
Epidemic genocide
From babies barely born
To a man who stood for pride
Addiction is affliction
Cured by love and not by hate
Opportunity and purpose
Not a brutal po-lice state.

How many more sweet babies
Strung out before they're born
How many Huey Newtons
By strife and conflict torn
How many generations
Before at last we see
An end to this affliction
Affliction of addiction
Through an end to poverty.

III.
Huey in the coffin
Elderly woman
Wails out loss
Pulls back the shroud
To kiss him one last time
Beneath the baptist cross.

Huey in the coffin
Tiny beautiful
Brown baby
'Cross the funeral aisle from me
Sweet young family mourns
What will baby's future be?

Huey in the coffin
Precious Lord Take My Hand
I cry, the man just next to me,
Rivulets of tears run down his face
But the feeling's not just grief
The real message is belief:

We do believe resistance to oppression
Like a mighty river, flows on
Though rapids may be perilous
And whirlpools treacherous,
The delta of struggle opens
Onto the Sea of Freedom.

IV.
Got the blues for Huey Newton, with a tragic beat
Got the blues for Huey Newton, with a tragic beat
Blown away in Oakland, yeh shot down on the street.

Police they say cocaine, and they say they got the guy
Police they say cocaine, and they say they got the guy
Gotta shake your head and wonder, why o why o why

Whatever way you slice it, bread still tastes the same
I said whichever way you slice it, the bread will taste the same
This was a man whose courage gave him no small share of fame

So no matter how they tell it, with undercover twist
Yeh, no matter how they tell it, with all their dirty twist
When a people meets oppression, that people will resist

Got the blues for Huey Newton, with a tragic beat
Got the blues for Huey Newton, with a tragic beat
Rose up from the ghetto, now returns unto the street.

KPFA at Full Moon

Full moon of Lunar New Year
Shine down wise eyes upon
This radio signal KPFA
This network Pacifica
To guide me as I write, and while
You're at it shed some light
Upon the legacy of Elsa Knight Thompson
Who, after all is said and done,
And regardless of all the acrimony surrounding her,
Did more than anyone to establish and sustain
KPFA and Pacifica as an authentic voice
An alternative vision, a listener-supported tone of truth.

"Failure to tell the truth," a bearded leader once said,
"Is an indication of a lack of faith in the future"
"The truth," said Elsa with a wry smile,
       "is always left of center!"
And even near the end she still said of this strange organism
This "far-out Berkeley radio station"
       (in the words of Ed Montgomery)
That had twice seen fit to guillotine her
"The whole is greater than the sum of its parts."
That is to say the "big idea" is greater than even
The blood sweat and tears of thousands of
Unpaid programmers; greater than all the distinguished names
Who learned some measure of their stature there,
Greater than all the board operators and community apprentices
Than the lack of splicing tape, (just one element in the
Incredible failure of most managements
To comprehend the actual hands-on work
That must go on; the short shrift given to production)
Greater than the injustices, the internecine conflicts,
The jealousies, rivalries, ego trips,
Political divisions, and sheer unremitting idiocies,
Greater than the repetitious Marathons, the dire diatribes,
The tone poems whose modernity
       is only equalled by their obscurity,
Yet and still, the whole is greater than the sum of its parts.

However, when something is rotten in Denmark
It cannot be ignored—the stench makes that impossible.
Just as in treasured Declaration of Independence, so too at
Free speech radio, "when a long chain of abuses" comes to light
The depth of the anger of workers and community is startling
No one denies that a station like this cannot please everyone
No one denies that there are those who'd like to see it sink
But that does not provide a license for mismanagement.

Pure democracy may only be a dream,
Yet practical democratic management,
Prior consultation of people affected, organizing for change,
Rather than trying to ram it from on high—that's the least
These talented and quite dedicated programmers
Deserve and demand.

And if it is not for the listeners and potential listeners,
      who are we for?
Not on the basis of Arbitron ratings,
      not to curry Foundation favor,
But instead to foster, explore, and ride the waves of change, for
The people are a river that never ends, and
Justice flows a mighty stream.

Full moon of Lunar New Year, may these lines
Reach into communities of change
And help them comprehend the ways KPFA
Can help them, find best ways to
      keep the station on the up and up
The times are difficult—they always are—once this station
Was a North Star inspiring us onward
Even in the worst of times, but now I simply have to say
The bright spots, flashpoints, fewer and more far between,
The News unlistenable and often worse than that
Betraying no real thought,
      no understanding of its great potential,
Trapped in an ill-advised effort to "cover" it all,
Leading with the same things as every other newscast
Burying even unusual or special interviews
Beneath a turgid tide of mediocrity and poor delivery.
True, there are good programs on KPFA
Many volunteers who strive creatively
Some real connections to communities
But what the station lacks is that special combination
Of compassion and curiosity that is journalism at its best
It lacks vision, political maturity, leadership
Perhaps confusing times are partly to blame
Station's soul shifted from radical blend, eclectic mix,
Embodied in volunteer programmers
To bureaucratic, Foundation-driven conservative centralism.
Some may argue this was inevitable in these times
Maybe so, but if things stay this way, it won't be too long
Before the main things we knew as KPFA are gone.

Confessional (2003)

I confess
I am guilty of—Love!

I confess
I have engaged in friendship.

I admit I have consorted with
All manner of people

Have tenderly touched—
Cats, dogs, lovers, flowers

Been guilty of marveling at
The stars, a stone, an autumn leaf

I acknowledge
I've committed crimes of kindness

Been implicated in
Acts of empathy and passion

Been convicted
Of having convictions

Conspired to
Breathe in better air

Gone underground
To pray with earthworms

Secretly plotted
To save the redwoods

Stand accused of harboring visions
Of evolution of our species toward justice and peace.

I confess
I am guilty of—Love!

Deep In My Heart

Deep in my heart I do believe
The words ring out
From We Shall Overcome
With gospel certainty
Her voice inspires
Awakens, sends
Beautiful, shivering
Vibrations up and down my spine
Deep in my heart I do believe
We shall overcome
Someday...

We will end Jim Crow
We'll walk hand in hand
We shall live in peace
We are not afraid
The whole wide world around
Deep in my heart I know that I do believe
We shall overcome someday...

Some way

These words
Still sing in my heart
After all these years
Somehow these words remain
As vital as ever
Still sing, still ring
Despite the loss and pain
These words still sing
Still signify
Roar a Malcolm
Soar a Martin King
Testify a Mahalia
Shout an Aretha
To the strength and endurance
Of the human spirit
To throw off bondage
Cut through the rope
These words still ring
Never to abandon hope
For it was said by an Emily D.
Hope perches in the soul and sings
And never stops at all.

For Miranda On Her 40th Birthday

From the high wooden backstairs on 14th Street
That you crawled up as I watched carefully
To the butternut tree on Osceola
That you climbed up long before me
From the gravelled rooftop theatre of 1070 Oak
Where "Big Joe" won his Freedom
To the schoolyard fence at Highland
And the meals you sneaked down to the basement
From the Fillmore to the Mission
Haight-Ashbury to Playland-at-the-Beach
Ukraine Bakery to Crystal Palace Market
That fresh-baked bread, that halavah.
Graphic Arts Workshop to People's World bazaar
Peters-Wright Dance Studio to Dudley Stone School
From the Panhandle to Holly Park
Junior Museum to Ocean Beach
There are places we remember
From all the places memory can reach
To all the lessons experience can teach
From me to you and you to me
With Love Love Love you in a place
Where there's all space and time,
Sister, comrade, friend of mine
From then to now—from life to death
From joy to grief—from root to leaf
From bad to worse to better best
From North to South to East to West
In everyplace I see your face
Smiling, laughing, strong, and free
Past tears and fears, through all the years
From childhood places we remember
To other lands, where tender
Blossoms of tomorrow open to the sun
And wherever you have gone
You have truly graced communities
With your precious presence
Bringing the walls to birth
Brightening the lives of all who "walk along together"
With color and meaning and affirmation
With energy, spirit, determination
For all of this, and so much else,
All the radiance and beauty you gift us with
All the intuition and understanding
You shower upon the world—
Your Rainbow of Love
All your powers of creation
All of this and so much more—
Attends this birthday celebration!

Song An Embrace for Chris   July 1991

song an embrace
of brotherly love
sung everyplace
below and above
sung to the stars
to roots underground
song an embrace
clinging singer to sound

song an embrace
child moments shared
through time and space
yet no one spared
trauma and pain
don't hush, do explain
song an embrace
clinging thunder to rain

song an embrace
a hug and a hold
through all the years
your birth to enfold
as sun and moon
dance ecliptical dawn
song an embrace
clinging gentle to fawn

song an embrace
for all who are gone
song an embrace
for all who live on
sung everyplace
below and above
song an embrace
of brotherly love.

For Meridel with All Love from Lincoln
February 1990

From whence
Arose that Voice?
Her vibrant voice —
Out of wildflowered prairies
Flowing Mississippis
Of masses in motion
Spreading in deltas
To oceans of Freedom.

From whence arose that Voice?
Her vital voice —
Out of picket lines and strikes
Protests, demonstrations
Street-corner orations
Struggles for justice and peace
Redeeming even the bloodiest century.

From whence arose that Voice?
Her clarion voice —
Out of a child's wonder
The treasured book
Celebrating heroic lives
Of people just like ourselves
Etched images of daily courage.

From whence arose that Voice?
Her Goddess voice —
Embracing Mother Earth
In global-village hug
Calling forth the sacred circle
Free women's choruses
Chant healing hosannas.

From whence arose that Voice?
Her radiant voice —
Full melodic moon, warm glowing sun,
Silken, fluid, sensual,
Viscous, flowing honey
Oozing golden-brown in cup of tea
From whence arose that Voice?

Deep desert springs
Ancient redwood rings,
Eagle-condor circlings
Clear measured cadences to keep us keeping on
Radical rhythms, solid, sure, and strong
Like some great gong
Heralding the communal dawn.

Meridel, your Voice rings out, sings out
Brings out the best in all of us
Your voice, rooted in the people,
Cradled in the corn,
Of Love and Labor born
In Liberty's sweet harmonies
Forever solidarities.

Rooted in the people
In flesh and blood and bone
In plant and star and stone
In truth and love and friends
Past obstacles, round bends,
The harvest comes, the flowering,
Your voice sings out empowering:

"The people are a story that never ends,
A river that winds and falls and
        gleams erect in many dawns;
Lost in deep gulleys, it turns to dust,
        rushes in the spring freshet,
Emerges to the sea.
The people are a story that is a long incessant
Coming alive from the earth in better wheat, Percherons,
Babies, and engines, persistent and inevitable.
The people always know that
        some of the grain will be good,
Some of the crop will be saved, some will return and
Bear the strength of the kernel,
        that from the bloodiest year
Some survive to outfox the frost."

The Present of Your Presence

The present of your presence
Is a gift to all concerned
For our presence in the present
As everyone has learned
Is the reason we are living
Is the gift that we are giving
Seasoned greetings fill the air
The present of your presence
Is a gift beyond compare.

Decade before the next millennium begins
Comets cavalcade the Universe, Earth spins,
Upon a tree of mulberry a fat worm weaves
A wondrous thread, transforms chewed leaves
Into a shining silken strand, the human hand,
Has learned to harvest the cocoon,
To sacrifice the pupal moth,
Creating cloth as luminous as moon.

Decade before the next millennium begins
Hunger stalks the streets, Earth spins,
Economies and nations reel in disarray,
Homeless and dispossessed, lives cast away,
So many sacrifice and still confusion reigns.
Yet chaos brings change wise ones explain
These tears are shed, as snake its skin,
We are not now what we have been,
Our interwoven efforts can be spread
Like delicate paintings on silken thread
Gifts of creativity and care to share, otherwise we
Stagger on surviving, oxen yoked to greed,
Like Taíno wove cotton for invaders of old
Enslaved to those few for whom God is gold.

Renew affirming and amazing graces
With big and little in near and far places
Connected with earthworm, as with stars of night,
For Palestine justice to reach the light,
Beginning this decade remember well
The paths we have taken, the people who fell,
Shining freedom for Leonard, Geronimo,
Sensing the essence of how plants grow
Wise native rootholds of original ones,
Footholds of those with great visions to come
Of a time when all people and beings of life
Will together abolish oppression's cruel strife
For a decade determined free growth to increase
And a long view to Justice, the sole path to Peace.

The present of your presence
Is a gift to all concerned
For our presence in the present
As everyone has learned
Is the reason we are living
Is the gift that we are giving
Seasoned greetings fill the air
The present of your presence
Is a gift beyond compare.

Mother's Day 1989

In another crisis in
My continuing battle with pain
I write

Do I believe in God? and answer

     Yes, if by God is meant the enduring energy and
equality of the human spirit, the intricately intertwining
lifelove rhythms of the universe, and the peace which
passeth all understanding.

(or as the Serenity Prayer says)

     God grant me the serenity
     To accept the things I cannot change
     The courage to change the things I can
     And the wisdom to know the difference.

(or as my father penned)

     Out of the curse of my poor birth
     From egg and sperm ill-fashioned
     Came this I of little worth
     As if by ghouls imagined
     Came visions of a Godliness
     That I cannot attain
     And dreams of errant loveliness
     That I profane...

Smelling the roses this spring
One with such an intoxicating scent
I kept coming back for more—it's called Voodoo...

Mother's Day 1989
My birthmother Anne
Lives on in the spirits
Of all who knew
Her compassionate energy
And shining love eyes
In her children and grandchildren.

Yet and still, I always cry, on Mother's Day.

Song for My Mother

It's been many years
Since she passed away
But I can still hear Mama say
When times were hard
And skies were grey
"Tomorrow is another day..."
     Chorus:
     Tomorrow is another day
     Is another way to say
     Though the times be sad and blue
     We have the strength to make it through

The years have flown
Swift soaring birds
Yet I can still hear Mama's words
As we wander on our way
"Tomorrow is another day..."
     Chorus

Sweet mother dear
Your lovelight shone
Now your children all have grown
When we feel low we hear you say
"Tomorrow is another day..."
     Chorus

Lullaby Blues (by Christopher Bergman)

Sleepy time don't come so easy
I feel I'm bound to lose
I feel I'm sliding down my rainbow
To the bottom of my blues

Don't go follow my example
Don't let the darkness cover you
'Cause I ain't seen no kind of darkness
That you couldn't shine right through

Now the wind it pulls me onward
I've got to go out for myself
But you know I'm only leaving
To find you somewhere else.

Palestine-Petalled

For Miranda and the Break the Silence Mural Project

Intifada
Palestine-petalled
Thunderous Intifada hooves
Miranda, Earthflower,
With Susan, Dina, and Marlene,
Resplendent in the energy
Of courageous creativity
And multi-petalled solidarity
Miranda, my sister,
She of the climbing,
She of the shining eyes,
The beautiful interweaving
Of the four sister-spirits

As red anemone of Palestine
Prepares to bloom
Olive leaves exude
The oxygen of peace...
Justice achieved stone-by-stone
No longer alone, the People
Awaken in Intifada of Freedom
Horse flares nostrils, muscles ripple
Hooves strike earth
Head raised victorious
Over cruelty and torture, as once
The fighters of the Warsaw Ghetto
Triumphed in spirit
Over Hitler's hated legions.

For who today the stormtroopers?
And who the people of the Diaspora?
Who the "people of the book?" —
Those who close down schools,
Or those who defy arrest and torture
Detention without charge
For simply teaching children
How to read and write?

Who the martyr?
The 16-year-old patriotic dancer
Image of grace
Shot down as he crossed the street?
Or the Ouzi'ed settler
Whose "final solution"
Sends shivers up and down
The spine of Justice?

Sing O Palestine
Sing O Tribes of Israel
Of the Peace of Justice
The only lasting peace, for
War need not be the only outcome

Yesh Givul: there is a limit
There can be a boundary
An end to this bestial
Ever more desperate denial
Of rights proclaimed
As those of every
Human being, every nation.

Yea, though the path
Ahead be strewn with thorns
And tempests whirl the desert
Though the Emperors pour
Soldiers, guns, and ammunition
Into the breach, the Spirit
In every human breast still beats
The stores close like clockwork
In general strike; the children
Carry folded-up flags in their pockets
The towns refuse to pay taxes
No Taxation without Representation
The world's vast majority
Recognizes their insistent call
The red anemone of Palestine
Prepares at last to bloom.

Sing Hallelujah, for when this happens,
Then and only then will these two peoples
Whose stories intertwine like cousins on the vine
Find true connection;
Achieve their fullest peoplehoods
And their children, oh so sweet,
Taste fruits of Liberty and Peace.

Intifada
Palestine-petalled
Thunderous Intifada hooves
Miranda, Earthflower,
With Susan, Dina, and Marlene,
Resplendent in the energy
Of courageous creativity
And multi-petalled solidarity

210

Miranda, my sister,
She of the climbing,
She of the shining eyes,
The beautiful interweaving
Of the four sister-spirits
Narrating the slide show
With the same sharing
Seen in every mural's magic

As for that one mural
That had to be painted in the dark
Until just before it was finished
Yet came out beautiful
Perhaps that is an apt,
If unfortunate, metaphor
For what is going on
In this non-evolved world of ours
Only grant that when at last
Light is shed upon our efforts
The historic results will also shine.

Shine like the
Red anemone of Palestine
Like the dancing light around
The graceful martyr
Shine like the eyes of Ethel Rosenberg
Like the energy of those who
Work together, Palestinian and Jew,
Perhaps now painting in the dark
But lighting a powerful spark
Shine like the reflection from
The tears in my eyes
As I begin to realize
The power and beauty of this art
The tremendous contribution
That has been made to

Intifada
Palestine-petalled
Thunderous Intifada hooves
Miranda, Earthflower,
With Susan, Dina, and Marlene,
Resplendent in the energy
Of courageous creativity
And multi-petalled solidarity
Miranda, my sister,
She of the climbing,
She of the shining eyes.

Persian Gulf Sonnet: January 20, 1991

The sonnet form goes back a long long time,
But can it comprehend the present day?
Tradition's rhymes and meters can't convey
The "surgical" detail of high-tech crime.
Perhaps a scream of pain would better serve,
Or roar of anger at such heinous acts,
For when the people add up all the facts
The truth will strike against a bitter nerve.
Now millions rise and chant for this war's cease
Huge demonstrations all around the earth
May these be prelude to long-needed birth
Of Justice, the foundation stone of Peace.
This sonnet's synthesizing final line—
The independent state of Palestine.

Persian Gulf Limericks

There was an Iraqi, Saddam,
To Kuwait he thought he could glom
Bush, scared for his oil,
Brought all Earth to a boil,
Will it explode like a bomb?

Who are these Sultans and Kings
Who wear ruby and emerald rings?
They ain't democratic
But feudal-fanatic
For their supper Georgie Bush sings.

Now this Georgie is hardly a saint
In fact that's the one thing he ain't
Vietnam to Grenada
Chile to Panama
His hands they are bloodily stain't.

All his words about freedom are lies
His rhetoric merely disguise
Oil, power, and wealth
Contracts for the Stealth
Throwing sand in his own people's eyes.

It's enough to make anyone sick
That so many still fall for this trick
From "Remember the Maine,"
To, "this man is insane."
They just want to swing their big stick.

Yeh, Georgie's got plenty to hide
Like his own CIA genocide—
For this rich Saudi king
He'll risk everything,
While waffling on apartheid.

This mild-mannered oilman from Hell
It is snake oil he's trying to sell
As recession cuts deep
We are taxed by this creep
Not to mention his son's S & L.

The media's got mud in its eyes
Drops of oil and blood on its ties
A cheerleading section
For this misdirection
The stuff they report catches flies.

So what if some millions are killed
If clinics with wounded are filled
Our children so sweet
Yet this cruel world they meet
When at last will war's evil be stilled?

And don't for a moment assume
That skin doesn't still call the tune
Vicious Arab-o-phobia
Feeds their megalo-globia
We're deluged by racist cartoons.

213

As far as the death toll will go
Who's up at the front we all know
More Blacks and more Browns
The first ones cut down
More than equal when blood starts to flow.

The invaders of the West Bank
Were not stopped by big U.S. tanks
Instead billions in aid
For bomb and grenade
Are the USA's way to say thanks.

Saddam might well be a swine
And his goals most surely not mine
But on this we agree
We both know there will be
A new nation named Palestine.

Disproportionate war preparations
When what's called for are negotiations
Bush had to rush in
Rocky swings for the chin
Overstepping the United Nations.

Thus they deal out the peace dividend
The juggernaut now gets to spend
Star wars, lasers, genetics
Nuclear pyrotechnics
Building weapons for war without end.

So down with the boast of top brass
Let's put people's lives before gas
Chanting, "Bring Home the Troops!"
Forming anti-war groups
Stopping war by joining en masse.

There's only one thing left to say
As was warbled by great Marvin Gaye
Their greed worse than cancer
War is not the answer
Let's bring in some peace here today!

Thanksgiving Day 1991

Thanksgiving Day dawns crisp and clear
For homeless under freeways in the doorways at
Soup kitchens featured on TV—boats leave San Fran
For Alcatraz, beacon of Native American resurgence,
Thousands gather, appropriate remembrance
Of the holiday's origins,
And celebration of the corn rebellion rising in 1992
On through the year 2000 and succeeding generations
May those to come indeed succeed in harmonizing
Their activities with the natural cycles
And may even we, beleaguered by the bestiality
Of private property, the grasp of greed,
Entrapped within the cruelty of desperate days
Bring forth upon these shores beginnings of wise ways.

Thanksgiving Day, at the Unitarian Church,
Poems from many cultures sing the praises
Of justice, peace, affirm the human spirit,
Gathered with friends, appreciating this
Sustenance, turkey and stuffing, when we know of so much need,
The children running happy at the playground,
The seasons turning once again, so soon, so soon
As time rushes by, overtaking everything,
We take the sacred moments when we can, we sing
Amidst the utter degradation, emmiseration,
Desperate depression and Bush-league regression
To all the worst clichés of capital in decline.
Gentleman with a family will work for food.
Amidst the arms sales spiralling, the irony of
Someone like Shamir importing settlers in to colonize
Against the backdrop of Hitler's "lebensraum" in
This same century, may next Thanksgiving find us
Active witness to real progress in the Middle East.

Meanwhile the city streets are filled with miseries
Miseducation, misappropriation of massive public funds
Stab deep in violent, twisted, sick scenarios of pain
My five year old asks why of poverty—who can explain
As Shakespeare had it—getting and spending we lay waste
Or Thoreau's mass lead lives of quiet desperation
Yet we know, and his and herstory confirm that
Great strengths reside within the people, whose force can be
Sudden, swift, and often irrevocable, sweeping
In new ways in days and hours with unimagined powers.

If our people fight one tribe at a time all will be killed
They can cut off our fingers one by one
But if we join together, we can make a powerful fist.
On this Thanksgiving Day may the wisdom
Of the original inhabitants hold special place
Within the heart; may the hands of those who
Tenderly nurtured the grass seed into corn
Creating thousands of varieties, encourage
An underlying unity, envisioned as a weave
From a diversity of souls and strategies, emerge
Blanket to warm and protect the best in each of us

Beautiful blanket, woven in practice and patience,
Bold in design, bright, textured, wondrous to
            the eye and touch,
Blanket to embrace the homeless, unemployed, dispossessed,
Spreads its artistry as signal of esteem
            to bright-eyed Native child
Whose stories go back perhaps to human genesis
Blanket to affirm the intricate weavings of all peoples
Patchwork quilts and calicos, silkscreens,
            paintings, tapestries,
The very fabric of our distinctive cultures and
            common humanity
The connecting thread that interleaves between us all
As Chief Sealth said, "the Earth does not belong to people,
People belong to the Earth.
All things are connected
Like the blood that unites one family
All things are connected."

May each of us, we the single threads, in our own lives,
With our own friends and families,
Give thanks, endure, somehow survive,
Mend and blend unique attributes of every hue and shade
Renew, revitalize ourselves to face tumultuous decade.

He Was the "First"

What does "Columbus" mean to me?
It does not mean "discovery"
It hardly calls for celebration
Nor praise of Europe's navigation.

What does "Columbus" mean to me?
It does not mean equality
Instead of truth and toleration
Duplicity and domination.

Columbus first of all you see
Put "Indians" in slavery
Shipped them to the shores of Spain
Traded lives for his own gain.

Columbus and his greed for gold
Scream horror stories yet untold
Do they deluge us in his fame
To cloak his ignominious name?

What does "Columbus" mean to me?
What is his place in history?
How many "Indians" were burned?
How many lies have we all "learned?"

What does Columbus mean to me?
A tragedy of savagery
It shakes the Spirit to the core—
He was the first Conquistadore.

Quincentennial Limericks

Columbus would never have sailed
If in measurement he had not failed,
He thought this round ball
A great deal too small
For this error he now is hailed.

There's something else that's much worse
For millions a terrible curse
Early journals are filled
With the Natives they killed
In conquest to fatten their purse.

If you had your purse on a chair
That I took as you turned unaware
You might call me a thief
I don't share your belief
I "discovered" your purse over there!

The people Chris met I must stress
Were people no more and no less
They were made into slaves
And soon filled up mass graves
Crimes to which none did confess.

One quite humane Spanish priest
Tried to record it at least
Las Casas his name
He called out the blame
Who indeed was the savage, the beast?

Conquistadores came and they went
Slaves, goods, and riches were sent
To Spain and the rest
Stuffing royalty's chest
For more war and conquest 'twas spent.

France and England got into the frays
Killing "Indians" up North a-ways
From a dinner of thanks
To blood-red river banks
Where buffalo no longer graze.

This is progress, so Europe proclaimed
Whole tribes were destroyed and defamed
The cross and the gun
Will convert every one
Towns after killers were named.

The cost of advance, some have said,
Though a shame that so many are dead
They just wouldn't play
The "American" way
Viewing white men with anger and dread.

Well, why not, said a wizened great chief
You trampled our lives and belief
All you wanted was things
Gold, silver, and rings
You brought Mother Earth endless grief.

Some think that it's all long ago
But tragic injustices grow
Alcatraz, Wounded Knee,
Poor health care, poverty,
Redress of distress deadly slow.

Reservations still seek to contain
A spirit that's ever maintained
May the wisdom of old
Final justice unfold
For Freedom cannot be restrained.

Rainforests hacked down in Brazil
Industry can't get its fill
Polluting the sky
As more species die
Birds caught in the latest oil spill.

There's no way that we here today
Can make all this pain go away
But we can learn the truth
And make certain our youth
Remember in meaningful ways.

The Next 500 Years

Thus begins the next 500 years
Indigenous spirits gather in tribes
Amidst the family of nations
With O so many tribulations
From Inuit to Iroquois to Inca
In Mogadishu, Sarajevo,
Port-au-Prince, Jerusalem,
And all points far and near
Poverty, oppression, disease, and fear
Yet spirit resistant through sorrow's tears
Beginning the next 500 years.

Let prayer rise free
That this new era be
Freed from racial tyranny
No longer scarred by slavery
Not rife with strife
Nor grasped by greed
Let prayer of our struggle send
A time when all will comprehend
The organism WE
The cycles of ecology
Our species able to turn a page
Evolve to a more equal stage
Our "indigenuity" can flourish apace
Our lives be lived with amazing grace
With the only bottom line compassion
For only from Justice can Peace be fashioned
An essential sense of human worth
In harmony with Mother Earth.

Thus begins the next 500 years
Indigenous spirits gather in tribes
Amidst the family of nations
With O so many tribulations
From Inuit to Iroquois to Inca
In Mogadishu, Sarajevo,
Port-au-Prince, Jerusalem,
And all points far and near
Poverty, oppression, disease, and fear
Yet spirit resistant through sorrow's tears
Beginning the next 500 years.

Freedom Is A Constant Struggle
JULY 4, 1992   (for many voices—as broadcast)

What is July the 4th to me
Hoopla and hypocrisy
An independent state declared
But what about nations already there?
The Iroquois confederation
The Seminole, Lakota nations
Choctaw, Diné, Possawatomi
Pomo, Paiute, Cherokee
As even today in New York harbor
They salute Columbus, that old robber,
Smallpoxed blankets and cavalry
What is July the fourth to me?

What is July the 4th to me
Hoopla and Hypocrisy
The words belied Equality
Amidst the scourge of Slavery
Yet spirituals contained a code
Directions on the Freedom Road
Harriet Tubman, Sojourner Truth
Teach their lives to every youth
Slaves rebelled from very first day
Constructed Underground Railway
Resistance to oppression is the key
To the best in our his and her-story

What is July the 4th to me
Women denied equality
Yet from Susan B. to Emma G.
Rising always to be free
All the unsung valiant ones
Whose stirring stories yet to come
From suffragettes to sisterhood
A force to fight for greater good
Meanwhile a woman's right to choose
Is beaten, battered, torn, and bruised,
By a Court some call Supreme
Injustice rising to a Scream
Yet rising forth for self-determination
The spark of women's liberation.

What is July the 4th to me
Hoopla and hypocrisy
The rich landholders then held sway
In many ways still do today
Unemployment on the rise
As is the volume of their lies
1 out of 10 in California alone
More and more without a home
They blithely say "recovery"
Midst rising tide of misery
Race, sex, and class—the lines are drawn
And yet resistance still lives on
Some think it faded long ago
But all the past just goes to show
That tyranny at last is spurned
With working hands the wheels are turned.

What is July the 4th to me
A time to learn from used to be
Recall repression's raging whip
'Gainst liberty and comradeship
From Reconstruction's harsh betrayal
Leaders murdered, beatings, jail
As today, Duke, Helms and Quayle,
Wag their bigotry like tails
McCarthyism's icy blast
Lessons learned from bitter past
Back back go back to times back then
Resist—so they won't come again.

What is July the 4th to me
The people's held down need to be
Fulfilled by full equality
The search for real community
Diversity and harmony
A multiculture symphony
People in all complexity.
What is July the 4th to me
The things they didn't teach at all
The people who just would not fall
Here's just a few, make your own list
Of other learnings we may miss:

Fast Drum Music....Planet Drum way underneath, but setting a beat.... (all voices back and forth)

The Iroquois contribution to the confederation of the colonies and the US Constitution

The slaveholdings and slave children of many of the Founding "Fathers"

Shay's Rebellion of farmers in Massachusetts, an attempt to further democratize the newly independent USA, later the Kansas Corn Rebellion, the Farmer Labor movement...

Denmark Vesey, Nat Turner, the men and women who led the early slave rebellions that were the real prelude to emancipation

Harriet Tubman's generalship in the Civil War, her and Frederick Douglass' alliance with John Brown, and the ties of the Abolitionists and the early women's movement

The women's movement itself, from its earliest matriarchal healing roots through Sojourner Truth and Susan B. Anthony, the movement for suffrage, strikes and demonstrations for economic equality still unrealized, the long and murderous road to reproductive choice, now so threatened, the struggle for true domestic equality, and all of the militant, glorious, outrageous, life-affirming cultural and social contributions of the Women's Liberation movement past and present.

The bringing of Irish and Chinese labor to build the railroads...the vicious exclusionary racism of early unions against Chinese in California

Labor's Untold Story: from general strikes, the Haymarket struggle for the 8 hour day, the women textile and garment workers, Centralia Washington commune, the Industrial Workers of the World, or IWW, organizing drives of the CIO...Mother Jones and Gurley Flynn...the role of the Communist Party and others in fighting racism in the South in the 30s and 40s. Labor's untold story.

The Bonus Army march of the unemployed to Washington DC at the depths of the depression.

The recurrent surges of strong anti-imperialism, from Mark Twain and many others who opposed the Spanish-American war and its conquests, to US labor's solidarity with Mexico's Pancho Villa, the movement in the 1920s against the US intervention in Nicaragua, the rarely-noted courageous resistance against the Korean war, then the millions who marched and organized against the war in Vietnam and all of Indochina...solidarity with Central America and Palestine...and all those who continue to resist the iron fist of the New World DisOrder.

The imprisonment of Japanese Americans in concentration camps and confiscation of their property during World War II...the atomic bombing of Hiroshima and Nagasaki, its continuing genocidal toll, and the current rise of anti-Asian prejudice...

Paul Robeson, WEB DuBois, Langston Hughes, Margaret Walker, the Harlem Renaissance... The foot soldiers of the civil rights and Black liberation movements, from the Student Non-Violent Coordinating Committee and the Montgomery Bus boycott, to Medgar Evers, the Deacons for Defense and Justice, Robert Williams, the Black Panther Party, all the rebellions, James Baldwin, Lorraine Hansberry, and the prophetic voice of Malcolm X, now echoing so powerfully over and over again.

The rise of new movements, consciousness and cultural vision from Latin American and Asian American communities.

The united farmworkers movement...

The rapid growth of the movement in solidarity with South African freedom...

The Cuban Revolution...the numerous U.S. invasions of Latin America... in Nicaragua past and present, in Panama and Grenada, the bloody Chilean coup, the overthrow of Arbenz in Guatemala, mistreatment of immigrant workers, refusal to grant asylum to Haitian and other refugees from tyrannies...

Give us "your tired, your poor,
Your huddled masses,
Yearning to breathe free"
What is July the 4th to me?

So many murdered and maimed, named and unnamed... Emmet Till, Joe Hill, Sacco and Vanzetti, Ethel and Julius Rosenberg, Martin and Malcolm, Fred Hampton, Viola Liuzzo, Cheney, Schwerner, and Goodman, the lynchings, the backstreet abortions, the assassinations and covert conspiracies.

The prison rebellions, from Attica to San Quentin...the political prisoners of today, Geronimo Pratt...Leonard Peltier... movements against capital punishment.

The Stonewall Rebellion and the powerful rise of gay and lesbian liberation, the battle against AIDS, new attitudes toward sexuality and family and the vicious reactions of the right wing.

The growing worldwide movement and awareness of the environmental emergency and the need to live in harmony with Mother Earth if we and all living things are to live at all.

Coming full circle, from the original beginnings of these continents, the resurgence of Native American wisdom, vision, and resistance from Alcatraz to Wounded Knee, struggles for treaty rights and sovereignty, and speaking the truth about the Quincentennial.

What is July the 4th to me
A time to share a prophecy

A time, as sixties songs did tell
To teach our children, teach them well...
As Howard Zinn said, in closing his
People's History of the United States:

> "People might create a new, diversified, nonviolent culture, in which all forms of personal and group expression would be possible. People...could then cherish their differences as positive attributes, not as reasons for domination. New values of cooperation and freedom might then show up in the relations of people, the upbringing of children.
>
> To do all that, in the complex conditions of control in the United States, would require combining the energy of all previous movements in American history—of labor insurgents, Black rebels, Native Americans, women, young people—along with the new energy of an angry middle class. People would need to begin to transform their immediate environments—the workplace, the family, the school, the community—in a series of struggles against absentee authority, to give control of these places to the people who live and work there.
>
> These struggles would involve all the tactics used at various times in the past by people's movements: demonstrations, marches, civil disobedience, strikes and boycotts and general strikes, direct action to redistribute wealth, to reconstruct institutions, to revamp relationships; creating — in music, literature, drama, all the arts, and all the areas of work and play in everyday life, a new culture of sharing, of respect, a new joy in the collaboration of people to help themselves and one another."

Music Under

You have been listening
To Freedom Is A Constant Struggle
Tonight featuring a special
Fourth of July program
Presented by Lincoln Bergman, Barbara Lubinski,
Heber, Kiilu Nyasha, and Nina Serrano,
with Kent Yeglin as engineer....
Tune in next Saturday at 6:30 for
Another edition of Freedom Is A Constant Struggle...

But don't leave yet
We're not quite done
We'll leave you with a ballad sung
By Paul Robeson
Written by Earl Robinson
To touch you with
This one last thought
Before the final bell has rung—
The greatest songs are still unsung:

END: Ballad for Americans: Record/Paul Robeson

Note: So the program closed with the powerful *basso profundo* voice of the great Paul Robeson, who I had the fortune and honor of meeting several times as a child, caressing the lyrics of the great radical labor singer Earl Robinson, a fighter and activist all his life who in later years became a dedicated environmentalist. For me, in the lyrics, a repeated refrain of Ballad for Americans resonates like a Freedom Bell:

**Especially the people,
That's America to me.**

*Especially the People!
That's the world around
to me!*

Rodney King and Me

They beat and beat the Black man down
We saw it on the screen
My mother gasped, my father cursed,
It was a shocking scene.
They said the man was dangerous,
But anyone could see,
There was no need to pound like that:
Police brutality.

They said his name was Rodney King
Battered and shattered was he,
An African-American
Like Rosa Parks and me
"It happens all the time," Pops said,
"But usually can be
Swept underneath the bloody streets
So no one else can see."

"But not this time," my Mama said,
And everyone agreed
Whoever made that video
Had planted a strong seed,
A seed like Langston told it
Planted in great need—
A picture worth a thousand words:
A Freedomseed indeed.

In school they praise democracy
And hail the Revolution
Patrick Henry's famous cry
And the U.S. Constitution,
All the documents and laws
Speak of equality,
But what does all this have to do
With Rodney King and me?

For it seems in Simi Valley
Just the other day
Twelve people dealt a verdict
That blew L.A. away.
My mother cursed, my father cried,
I felt myself turn sad inside,
Turn sad and mad, feel bad inside—
The camera could not have lied.

A history teacher told me
This nation's original sins
Of genocide and slavery
Were no way to begin
Great Native American peoples
Faced 500 years of death,
Kunta Kinte, his sisters and brothers,
Held in chains till their last breath.

Langston called it the rock
Where America stubbed its toe
The slave trade and its aftermath
Was not so long ago
Its bitter brutal legacy
Of lynchings, Klan and hoods,
Lives on in Simi Valley
And in many neighborhoods.

The country explodes in anger,
The streets boil over in rage,
A flaming violent volcano
Burns history's bloodstained page.
Bush preaches law and order
Brings his gunmen to the fray
Pays little lip service to justice
As he loots our lives away.

At the high school, they had a walkout
Marched down to City Hall
Cheered some powerful speeches
Then some smashed up the Mall;
It was raging, flaming anger
Strong but unorganized,
As Los Angeles burned before us—
I saw tears in my parents' eyes.

See, my parents went down to Selma
Mississippi Summer too
My mother arrested seventeen times
To gain rights for me and you
They often talk of "the movement,"
When all eyes were on the prize,
No matter how difficult times may get
They say new struggle will rise.

At a rally over in Oakland
I heard Angela Davis say
Although our rage was righteous
It soon would fade away.
How can the spark of resistance
She asked us, be maintained?
How can we build and organize
So the spirit will be sustained?

I look at the streets around me
Unemployment, frustration, crack,
Poverty's desperate cycle
The economy's broken back
I look at the people around me
Lack of health care, no respect
For young or old or in-between
All suffer from neglect.

I sit with my mother and father
In front of the TV,
Listen to Rodney King himself
Speaking haltingly:
In a voice choked with emotion
This victim of slavery's whip
Speaks of eventual Justice,
Says we're all on the same ship.

In a way we're all in it together
I know that can be true,
But it sure is hard to believe it
When people act like they do,
When twelve in Simi Valley
Kiss Pharoah's steel-toed feet—
But I think of the story of Moses,
And why Mary need not weep.

I'm young but no Pollyanna,
Yet not pessimism's child,
I know that needed changes
Don't come in meek and mild,
I believe in the power of People
And the spirit of Freedom song
I remember Martin's vision
And Malcolm's lessons strong.

It's gonna take time and trouble
Before Justice fills the courts
More schools, libraries, hospitals,
Not guns, or bombs, or forts,
It's gonna take hardship and sacrifice,
Death and destruction too,
But *deep in my heart I do believe*
More of the dream can come true.

Meanwhile I chant with my poems
Sing the Simi Valley blues,
Listen and learn and do what I can
To go out and make some news.
I'm sometimes up and sometimes down,
For we all need a friendly boost
And the last line belongs to Malcolm:
"The chickens come home to roost."

Moon Over Mandela   5/92

I.

Moon over Mandela
Bars don't block the view
Moon over Mandela
Shines free for me and you

Leader of a people
Long denied liberty
Their struggle is turning
His jailhouse key

And the people
Gather strong for freedom
No time for those who say "go slow"
The people gather strong for freedom
Apartheid it must go!

Moon over Mandela
Bars can't block the view
Moon over Mandela
Shines free for me and you.

II. Jump Rope Rhyme

Nelson Mandela
He's a great fella
I wanta tell ya
'Bout Nelson Mandela

He fought for our Freedom
Yes, that's why we need him
The other day they freed him
And yesterday I see'd him!

Nelson Mandela
Nelson Mandela
I wanta tell ya
'Bout Nelson Mandela.

III.

The other night
As I marvelled loudly
And repeatedly
At how Mandela's
Wisdom and truth-telling
Stood up to the
Slime of the U.S. media
Cheering him on
My three-year-old daughter
Commented:
"I think you're falling in love
With Nelson Mandela."
Of course, and as usual,
She called it perfectly.

IV.

Echoes of Shakespeare
With throbbing African beat
In the moving poetry of Mandela
Opening his speech to the U.S. Congress:

The human condition—
The individual is
Like a meteor that
Flits across the human stage
And passes out of existence
But the people are noble and heroic
They endure, multiply, are permanent
Rejoicing in the expectation and knowledge
That their humanity will be reaffirmed and enlarged
By open and unfettered communion with
The nations of the world.

Thank You Spike!

For Malcolm, Betty, Spike, Denzel
I sing this song today
For Ossie Davis, Ruby Dee,
And all they have to say
All actors and technicians
Who had a part to play
For Nelson and the children
And for Billie Holiday
For Jimmy Baldwin, Arnold Perl,
All others on the way
Who brought to birth this lasting work
Of Freedom's bright display
Who crafted from Black Shining Prince
And racist tragedy
A vision for the ages
Of what we all can be.

Yes, I see Brother Malcolm
Beaming from the screen
Reaching out and teaching
All the Truth can mean
Reaching out and teaching
With an eloquence so rare
A lesson for tomorrow
For all of us to share
Revolution's message
To go beneath the skin
To see below the surface
To where our bonds begin
To break the chains that bind us
To struggle to be free
Yes, I see Brother Malcolm
As we reach Equality.

Don't be hoodwinked
Don't be taken
Trust your own integrity
Hear the words
But watch the actions
Of the ones who claim to be
The leaders of tomorrow
Guardians of your liberty
Lest your future fill with sorrow
Brought on by their trickery
Of the people, by the people,
For the people may it be—
That Justice bloom and flower
From sea to shining sea
Wake up to "fight the power"
And make real Democracy!

Note: While Spike Lee's portrait of the life of Malcolm X
fails in some important ways to convey the revolution-
ary and internationalist synthesis of ideology and prac-
tice that Malcolm came to embrace—and can be criti-
cized from several other standpoints—it is nonetheless a
valiant attempt to educate, to tell the story, to pass les-
sons on. In this sense, and also in tribute to the stunning
and cinematically original contributions of Mr. Lee to
our artistic and cultural understanding, most especially
in "Do the Right Thing," and aware of the genius it takes
to bring together and direct such productions in this
gigantically corporate day and age, I say, "thank you."

When Eddie Marshall Plays...

When Eddie Marshall plays the recorder
Oh, then the air is blue and bright
And worlds collide in fancy flight
When Eddie Marshall plays the recorder.

When Eddie Marshall plays the recorder
Ma Rainey, Bessie, Lady Day
Just shake their heads to hear him play
It's Dixieland, bebop, and blues
Sojourner Truth and Langston Hughes
Hip-hop entwines with Lester Young
Songs are sung and Spring is sprung
When Eddie Marshall plays the recorder.

When Eddie Marshall plays the recorder
Africa meets Arab themes
Spirituals dance with Cuban dreams
Freedom flute flings wide all doors
Tide rolls on near and far-flung shores
The spirit soars like bird in flight
Oh, then the air is blue and bright
When Eddie Marshall plays the recorder.

Hey now, it's all of that, and then some,
When Eddie Marshall plays the drum.

Does Santa Believe? 1992

Santa's elves were in a tizzy
Was he sick? Did he feel dizzy?
They didn't know, they couldn't tell
Did someone cast an evil spell?
He said he wouldn't fly his sleigh
That Christmas could just go away
He said they all could stop their work
Shook his head, turned with a jerk
Yanked on his beard, rolled down his sleeves,
Said, "The problem is, folks, that I just don't believe,
I try and I try, but I just don't believe
I see all the toys, hear cash registers ring,
But deep down there is nothing to which I can cling
On my flight I can't leave if I just don't believe."

"He doesn't believe?" said Rudolph to an elf,
"How can Santa Claus not believe in himself?"
"I'm afraid that's not it," gasped the elf with a sigh,
"If I'm not mistaken, I think I know why,
Santa's so listless, so grouchy and mad,
I know just the problem that poor Santa has
If he doesn't get better the whole world will grieve—
It's in CHILDREN that Santa just does not believe!"

"But there's millions of children all over the world
He gets all those letters from boys and from girls."
"That's true," said the elf, "but it does make you wonder,
If pirates wrote letters to get all their plunder—
The letters seem sweet, just flowing with honey
But so many of them are all about money
All about fancy, expensive big gifts
And that's what's sent Santa down in the snowdrifts,
The way to return him to the land of the living
Is to search for some children who really are giving."

Luckily for the elves (and of course for us all)
Someone told Santa about Sara Small
Who helped to save dolphins by writing a letter
So big fishing boats would learn to fish better,
Then on the world network video screen
Someone showed Santa a quite touching scene
"Look closely at this," said an observant elf,
"A Somalian girl, thin and hungry herself,
Gives her last spoons of rice to her sweet little sister,
When you visit there, Santa, make sure not to miss her,
Leave enough food for ten years or more
Then set up a system of rainstorms galore!"

It was just at that moment, like a call of the wild,
Yet somehow so gentle, tender, and mild,
That Santa sat up, felt his own inner child,
And laying a finger aside of his beard,
And giving a nod, he said, "That's really weird,
I felt really sad, I was down in the dumps,
But the spirit of children my spirit has cheered
Right in the place where my Santa heart pumps—
Now I simply can't wait for those reindeer to jump!"
So he sprang to his sleigh, to his team gave a whistle,
And away they all flew, like the toe on a mistle,
We heard him exclaim, as he soared out of sight,
"I believe in the child, and now I'm all right."
In the distance he shouted, that jolly old sprite—
"May your Kwanzaa, your Hanukah, Christmas be bright
May you share Tribal Solstice 'round fires alight
With wishes for New Years of Health and Delight!"

Valentine's Day, inspired by Cricket

Love between equals is true romance.
Valentine's Day, Valentine's Day
As the winds of change
Pump through our hearts
Valentine's Day dawns clear and bright
The sunshine of the past few days
Evokes first cherry blossoms
An air of Spring
Yet Love is for all Seasons
Valentine's Day, Valentine's Day
But last night how many
Husbands beat their wives?
How many date rapes?
How many forced entries
Veiled threats, raised arms
Explosions of anger
That stopped just short
Of beatings, but filled so
Many hearts with fear?

Valentine's Day, Valentine's Day
What better day for us to say
That so long as
Violence and intimidation
Within relationships
Stay as American as apple pie
So long as the threat of force
Hangs over the marriage bed
Like a bloody guillotine
So long as women are afraid
To walk around their block at night
Then there really cannot be a
Valentine's or any other day
Devoted to love, of whatever variety,
Because true romance consists
Of love between equals.

Equality means mutual respect
Understanding, tolerance, forgiveness,
The right to be—and to be either in or out
Of any relationship based on
One's own free will, one's volition,
Not based upon a sense of duty
Or having one's arm twisted
Or in any other way being forced
To be with someone who
Mistreats, beats, or abuses,
Or who for any other reason you
At this time do not choose to choose.

Love between equals is true romance
And until the time when we can
Confidently say that violence
In relationships is a thing of the past,
Then at its best Valentine's Day
Can serve as day for us to gather and affirm
The gentle side, as gentle-men to speak,
Today perhaps a rivulet, a tiny creek
But tomorrow and tomorrow
May we grow into a river of love
A mighty Mississippi of women and men
Of all predilections and persuasions
An Amazon of amazing amplitude
Across the vast spectrum of emotion
A Nile of nearness, of feelings expressed,
A Yangste, Mekong, Congo, Volga
Danube, Seine, and Thames
Of learning how to give and to receive
Great rivers of people capable of change
Whose relationships still will sometimes see
Anger, discord, and misunderstanding
Blues and bad news
But will be free of all physical
And psychological abuse
Open to peaceful currents of communication—
My friends that would be cause for celebration
As glowing as the Sun that shines
As shining as the Moon that glows
When we exchange our Valentines
When equals meet and true love grows.

Harvest Time

Going through
All my poems and papers
Is overwhelming

So moved by all the messages
Of love
Made nostalgic by the
Resistant spirit

Seeking a way through it
Organizing principle
But more than that—

A harvest
That neither romanticizes
Nor belittles
That worldwide wave
Of which my poems
Are but an atom.

Red Diaper Baby

—such a background
continues to provide, I think,
a cultural bedrock,
a song, a mural, a poem
a connection to the poorest
and most oppressed
a strong sense of justice
passionate sincerity
irreverence and laughter
lots of love to give and receive

so,
even though
such a background
also has other
more negative, traumatic,
and wounding aspects.

I like to think
I led a truly happy childhood.

The five of us
The feeling of family
Extended outward
Connecting to
Progressive folks.

Together we shared
Vision of world transformed
By revolution.

Family tree
Spreading branches
Rooted in
Shared vision of
Deep passion for
Freedom and Peace.

For Anna on Her Batmitzvah

For Anna on this day I bring I sing:
The deepest currents of genetic rivers
Flowing from ancestral dawn –
Cave mother cuddling cradling child,
Chanting dancing wild at harvest moon,
For Goddess of Fertility,
Continents uplifted, famine, flood;
Mass migrations, sweat and blood.

For Anna on this day I bring I sing :
The ancient visions, legends, prophecies,
The people gathering to plot rebellion,
Smash slavemaster's chains; win freedom,
Wandering in deserts of despair and pain;
Rising in resistance to oppression
Scattered seeds in winds that blow,
That will take root, if nurtured, grow.

For Anna on this day I bring I sing:
The midwives, healers, merchants, serfs,
High priests, mystics, atheists, artists,
Seamstresses, tinsmiths, teachers, reachers,
The Esthers and Elijahs who
Rose on Warsaw Ghetto barricades,
A love of life's delights and learnings,
Yearnings for new and better days,
The mysteries of the human soul,
Infinite wonder of stargaze,
Universe in a grain of sand,
The healing power of the hand.

For Anna on this day, most of all, I bring I sing:
The passing on of empowerment and peace, passing on
From generation to generation, redwood ring to ring,
The transmission of the limited wisdom of the species
The unity and diversity of life, the spiritual center of belief
The energy and drive to do; ability to work
To make your dreams come true.

For Anna, the curtain opening, new act beginning, may it hold
A growing inner strength and beauty as the years unfold
Rising woman-tall among us all,
Coming of age upon the human stage,
A gorgeous blossom bursting free upon our human family tree.

A tree within whose capillary veins flows love
Whose roots and branches sing your praise
Leibel, my father, whose rebellious Talmudic love of Justice
Beats its own new rhythms in your relentless logic,
My mother, Anne, whose compassionate spirit
Daily brings me so much tenderness and creativity
Who visioned a time when the love of justice and truth
That is early youth would usher in a world for all to share
She lives in us, your ways with little ones, big sister care,
For it is never the children who make war.

For Anna and your growing role upon the human stage,
In your own inimitable style, for there are multitudes of ways,
Be the journey one of Justice toward Peace
In Palestine, Iraq, the Middle East,
South Africa, El Salvador, just down the street,
That longed-for feast of rainbow reconciliation
Between diverse peoples; global triumphs over
Poverty, racism, hunger, ignorance, discrimination of all kinds,
Shelter for the homelessness of body and of spirit,
Real progress in healing the dreaded diseases of our times,
Great collective collaboration in the creation of beauty and art,
In the dangerous and glad daily living of one's life part.

Anna, whatever your changing roles may be,
Whatever choruses your voice shall grace,
I know you know you carry with you all our love,
The indomitable spirit of extended family and friends,
Whose spreading branches help to see us through.
Whatever path you take, may it be true to you,
And may you, as those native to these lands, might say:
Always walk in beauty, reverence, serenity, and joy,
Treasuring the connectedness of all living things,
The spiritual strengths within yourself,
Nourished, given sanctuary, by the branches of the tree of life,
Resilient, healing, learning through the storm and strife.

My poems, Anna, are, as you well know, my deepest art
The only way I have to sing, to bring ,
What's in my heart—
So all that's left for me to do
Is say forever I love you.

Batmitzvah Sonnet
for Maia from Lincoln

A centered energy that glows so bright
Illuminating all with steady grace
The Moon, serene and full, alights the night
As now, in womanhood, you take your place.

From ancient Mayan subtle grasp of time
To modern Gaia theories of our Earth
The Sun and Moon in circling couplets rhyme
To celebrate your passages and worth.

From early worlds of mermaids you have grown
Now future efforts beckon rainbow-new
Imagination takes on flesh and bone
Creative powers to make dreams come true.

Bless her tomorrows, Sun and Moon above,
With joy and health and lots and lots of Love!

Sonnet to Mark on His 50th Birthday

It seems like only yesterday when we
Did joyously debate in academe
Time spins around its axis dervishly—
A constant Change its one and only theme.
Diverse intensities the years beget,
So much elapsed since we at Cornell roomed,
It seems like only yesterday, and yet,
Your plant of century is halfway-bloomed!
As Justice is the lasting key to Peace
And Wisdom only grows in Error's Earth
So Love and Friendship praise great mysteries
Compassion marks the path to Human Worth.
In rising beauty of Yosemite
Consider this a birthday poem from me.

Leaves of Love (for Leib Roscoe Lyman Sutcher)

Here's to Leib—
Of egg and seed
Child of giving
Light of living
Who will be fed
On milk, then bread,
In tender scenes
(Not by Marines).

Here's to Leib
Who'll want and need
To grow and know
From head to toe
Who'll churn to learn
In hands-on mode
Like leaf on tree
Leib will grow free.

Here's to Leib
For *lieb* means Love
As years may flow
He'll come to know
That people reap
Just what they sow
Deep in my heart I do believe
That Leib will be so great to know

Like brother Saul, or Jacquey, Steve
These things I really do believe
That Leib will take his right-full place
Upon this globe of human race
Of birds and bees and manatees,
Flowers, algae, redwood trees,
For *lieb* means Love and it's been found
Love can make world go round!

O child of Mogadishu dust
Who stares out asking whom to trust
Or child caught in cruel ethnic war
Who only seeks her own front door
For all of these sad suffering ones
And for the much more fortunate sons
Like they who run near San Fran Bay
Watch caterpillars, laugh, and play

For every child on every shore
That's who these lines of Love are for
As everyone in Earth's embrace
Welcomes now his special face
Shouts out to Leib to creep then leap,
Crow at the sky, sleep peaceful sleep,
Here's to Leib, and Love, and Birth
As children come to claim the Earth

A little child, 'twas said, will lead them,
To days of plenty, Peace of Freedom,
Leaves of Love on Trees of Share
Roots reach deep to places where
Rootholds of the soil can sing
Of the joys that life can bring
To celebrate this day of Birth
Upon Our Sacred Mother Earth.

Tutsi/Hutu (to the tune of Twinkle, Twinkle, Little Star)
Twinkle twinkle Freedom star   How I wonder where you are…

Tutsi, Hutu, blood and hate
Why can't people share their plate
Why can't people live in peace
Hutu, Tutsi, murder cease.

No more hatred based on race
No more killing any place.

Tutsi, Hutu, all be free
Have a right to liberty
Hutu, Tutsi, all are one
Walking equal in the sun.

No more hatred based on race
No more killing any place.

Tutsi Hutu murder cease
Huti, Tutsi, live in peace.

To Irving Fromer on his 80th Birthday
(variation on a theme by Nazim Hikmet)

Eighty years—If you ask the Universe
It will say, "Eighty years —
Sorry, I can't comprehend
Such an infinitesimally small amount of time."
If you ask a butterfly
It will say, "Eighty years —
Seems an eternity to me..."

The year you were born
The century had just begun
World War I seethed below the surface
Now, countless conflicts later
In what Meridel has called
The bloodiest of all centuries
Mother Earth still trembles under the
Threatening tyrannosaurus
Footsteps of nuclear nightmare
Environmental devastation
Greed and brutal exploitation.

Still, the Earth has gone round the Sun
Eighty more times—no small feat in itself
The apple trees still blossom
The foals yet rise on
Trembling legs to greet the dawn.
And me, remembering that time of course
When you taught me to draw a horse!

Life goes on, as Seeger sings,
"How do I know my youth is all spent
My get-up-and-go has got up and went
But in spite of it all I'm able to grin
To think of the places my get-up has been."

Eighty years—almost 30,000 days
Days of struggle, weal and woe,
So full they seem, so soon they go,
Maybe life and work are something like
Those statues of Michelangelo
Hewn from huge blocks of marble
From each a partly-sculpted figure
Struggles to emerge; they say he claimed
That he did not create the works
For which he's known
Rather that he simply used
His tools and sweat to bring forth shapes already there
Who were imprisoned in the stone.

Or perhaps today we'd say
That form and content interplay
Dialectically intertwine
In tension drawn of space and line
In mine and field and graphic arts workshops
We plant and plough and harvest crops
In stone, on canvas, on printed pages
Fashion from our part of rock of ages
Visions of what is and what can be
Draw Freedom's shapes—to set them free!

With power of your line and art
The lift of light, the hand and heart
The working class, the freedom song,
The leaflet's call, in union strong
You now become an octogenarian
But through it all a proletarian
A cultural worker, whose tools of the trade,
Are brush and pencil and light and shade,
For all oppressed who will be free
Your craft calls forth equality
Lifeworks, lifelines, they all ring true
True as my love and strength to you.

But enough of all this deep reflection
A toast to art and true affection
Down with "aesthetic" cerebration
The occasion calls for celebration
The relativity of time
Is not the reason for this rhyme
Instead it is my way to say
Happy Eightieth Birthday!

Note: I was honored that this poem appeared with others in the
printed program at the memorial celebration for this great artist.
Irving Fromer and his wife Katherine, who died several years before,
were warm, dedicated people—she a superb early childhood educator,
he a graphic artist whose energy and zeal seemed infinite. Our families
were close during the growing-up years—we shared a time of struggle
and awakening no one has yet succeeded in describing fully. And yes,
Irving taught me how to draw a horse in the Saturday morning
Graphic Arts Workshop class I attended with my sister and brother.
That day he taught me the essence of radicalism—as Marx said, to be
radical means to go to the root of things and at the root of things are
people themselves. Irving's lesson was an artistic one. I yearned to
draw a horse. He praised my fledgling efforts, then brought over a
book with a drawing of a horse's skeleton. He told me to draw that, in
pencil, which I did, very carefully. Then he came over, praised it, and
turned the page to a drawing of the horse's muscles, telling me to draw
them, erasing the skeleton beneath as needed. I did that—Irving came
over and said, "now draw the horse."

Seasonal Greetings   12/14/93

I.
Simply a few words
Seasonal greetings
That at best
Would apply to
Every day of our lives
Emphasize
Shared moments
Of working together
Appreciation for
Each other's gifts.
For it seems to me
That we all hold each other up
Weave of human need
Web of ebb and flow.

II.
How can a world that recognizes
And is capable of being ennobled by
Inspirational genius of Morrison or Mandela
A world of poetry, music, friendship, freedom, love
Tolerate the sheer idiocy of urban life—
Allow incessant violence and senseless starvation
Introduce sweet innocent children, as a matter of necessity,
To fear, distrust, and nightmare cruelty?
How can a world zany and irreverent as Zappa
A world humored by the likes of Tomlin or Chaplin
Exist amidst high schools banning baggy pants
Because guns are easier to conceal in them?
How, I ask you, how?

III.
Under the philosophic, changing night
The stars look down upon us, seeking
Sparkle, right-back-at-cha, from our eyes,
Glory in the Moon and Sun, their set and rise
And yet and still, defensive, under the night,
Our world in chaos lies,
Masking insecurity with bravado or passivity
Medicating epidemic depression and masking pain—
Where then dear ones, the affirming flame?
That centered warmth, bright laughter in the air,
The stirring of stomach butterflies before the play begins
Magnetic glance, hand held, poem shared,
If there be affirming flame, we find it there.

Delicious Flan   for Lisa   2/24/94

The delicious flan you made
At the end of a
Typically aggravating workday
In the midst of a
Particularly stressful week
Icing on the cake of your spirit
Emblematic of your special way
Resilient, affirmative, striving, compassionate,
The unique 40-year-old who is you
Or, as our inimitable daughter put it,
When critiquing a beauty pageant,
And I approvingly quote her word for word:
"Mom, those women are too thin—you're perfect!"
Images of ourselves in children's eyes
Naturally more truthful and direct
Indeed you are perfect as you are
The unique 40-year-old who is you
Perfect as cat sitting sphinx-like
Beneath cradling crescent Moon
As turtle meditating with steady gaze
Perfect as the
Heart-shaped drop of amber
Perfect as the
Delicious flan you made.

So may this heart of amber
Wherein beats the love of ages
Teach us to cherish each new dawn,
Yes, even every monthly cycle,
To welcome each new year
With body mind and heart soul
And may your days to come
Be filled with emotional growth
Bring rest and renewal and fulfillment
Along with all the dreams you dare to dream.

Just wanted to say
How much I appreciate you
And all the things you do
These forty lines of love
Are just my way to say:
Happy 40th Birthday!

The Redwood Anthem
(sung to the tune of Beethoven's Ninth)

Spreading wide with roots to river
Rising tall, red, brown, and green,
Toward the sky of starry splendor
Mighty redwoods stand serene.

They were here when tribal peoples
Told their stories, sang their songs
From those days trees still remember
They've seen all our rights and wrongs.

Ancient seers of our great forest
Ferns beneath your shaded brow
How can they cut down your beauty
Why can't they see reason now?

May your forests live forever
May your ecosystems thrive
Every redwood in the forest
In our hands can still survive!

Spreading wide with roots to river
Rising tall, red, brown, and green,
Toward the sky of starry splendor
Mighty redwoods stand serene.

Note: The main melody of Beethoven's Ninth was also used
as an anthem to human solidarity sung by Paul Robeson,
Pete Seeger, and others that I learned as a child. This poem
was inspired by my proofreading of a book by Dwight
Willard, on the Great Sequoia, those giant elders of our life-
family. In addition to marveling at Dwight's encyclopedic
collection of information about all the groves, I was struck
by his original and compelling proposal that each and every
Sequoia should be viewed as an individual rare plant, and so
protected in every possible way. This poem is also dedicated
to Rachel Carson, to Judi Bari, and to all radical environmen-
talists, opponents of toxic racism, and passionate protectors
of our Mother Earth worldwide. Movements for environ-
mental justice must become militant millions if our Earth is
to be sustained for our children's children—seven genera-
tions and more hence—children who we have a planetary
responsibility to love and cherish.

The Great Global Warming Limerick Debate

"The topic's a hot one at that,"
Said the first, putting on his straw hat,
"Evidence it is forming
That this globe is warming"
And the sweat dribbled down his cravat.

His opponent, unflappably cool,
Said, "please don't take me for a fool-
If the temperature's rising
It isn't surprising
It goes up, then goes down, as a rule."

"Sure, cycles exist," said the first,
Gulping water to stave off his thirst,
"But our excess pollution's
A new contribution
For this reason, I fear the worst!"

"Just put all your worries on ice,"
Said the other, tossing some dice,
"I'd much rather wait
Take my chances with fate
Till the bill is due, why pay the price?"

The outcome my friend's up to you
To find out which side is more true
Before more time passes
Analyze all the gases
And help figure out what to do.

Note: This is one of many poems written to accompany inquiry-based, hands-on activities in math and science published by the Great Explorations in Math and Science (GEMS) program at the Lawrence Hall of Science. I was Principal Editor and am now Associate Director of GEMS, which has achieved a nationwide reputation for educational excellence, teacher friendliness, and fun. This poem appears in *Global Warming and the Greenhouse Effect,* copyright by The Regents of the University of California and used here with permission. Many of these poems appeared in the GEMS publication entitled *Once Upon A GEMS Guide: Connecting Young People's Literature to Great Explorations in Math and Science.*

Turtle Island Mother Earth

To begin with there was no earth, only water,
With animals who swam or flew nearby–
Then there came a wondrous human Daughter
Who fell down from a torn place in the sky.
She needed soil of earth, or she would die.

Two Loons cried out and caught her as she fell,
Called for the other animals to lend a paw,
Set her to rest upon a giant Turtle's shell,
Began to dive into the Sea's vast craw,
To seek the earthly soil with tooth and claw.

The Beaver tried, his broad tail slapped the tide,
A Muskrat lent his whiskers to the search,
When they came up the Turtle looked inside
Their mouths to see if they had captured any earth.
Others tried and failed, returned to their sad perch.

Poor Toad stayed down so long he almost died,
But in his mouth, so deep the Toad had dived,
Turtle found a mound of earth (Toad glowed inside)
The wondrous Daughter of the sky survived!
She patted earth around the Turtle's shell, revived!

The soil began to grow and grow, becoming land,
Earth grew and grew upon Great Turtle's shell,
From clumps and countries continents expand.
Then Woman brought forth Children, with their Truths to tell,
Maize, beans, and pumpkins sprout from Her as well.

So Children of today, please listen as we say
That this Daughter from the sky created our Life's way
And were it not for the animals, the Loons and the Toad,
Who knows what might have happened on Life's long road
It's still a question, a mystery—
                  If not for that Turtle, where would we be?

Note: The above poem is loosely but respectfully based on a modified version of a Huron creation story, and appears in various forms in a number of other Native American traditions. It was published in the GEMS teacher's guide *Investigating Artifacts*, copyright by The Regents of the University of California, and used here with permission.

30th Anniversary of My Mother's Death

I.
These thirty years
Condense into
An overwhelming sense of loss
Even as on this very day
Darling clever Caitlin
Loses her first tooth!

Searching for the truth
To tell on the mountain
The human experience
Life and death
Cycles of love
Parabolas of pain

Even as Meridel ebbs then resurges
Creates the world again in her great way
All the ties of tenderness
Struggle, courage, family
Visit me this day.

II.
Nearly half a century
My scrawls and scrolls
Yet so much held
Somewhere inside
Within the pain
Embedded in the sorrow
Is an opening
A flow
I know
Nearly half a century
Can it be
That I have begun
To acquire
My modest share of wisdom?

III.
Not too long ago
Caitlin and me
Visited my mother's grave
I got a little lost
Caitie insisted we go on
Until we found it
We left some flowers
Said a few words
Spoke of planting a rose bush.
Thirty years ago today:
Only a few weeks
Before Miranda's birthday
A few months before Chris's
How unbearably hard
It must have been for her to leave
How wracking the pain
We were all good children
The loss of "Ma"
No words can explain
Our giving caring mother
No longer there—
Too much too much to bear.

IV.
Yes, we went on
Mistakes we made our share
Yet we created, loved, and cared
Helped others to see
The compassionate connection
That can grow from tragedy
Drawn together by the trauma
The warm weave of family
And by the changing times
Then later by our father's
Difficult, outrageous demise
And now we stand
Wounded yet sturdy
"Just like a tree
That's standing by the water"
Two sons and a daughter
Each of us growing
Making our way
Each of us knowing it was
Thirty years ago today.

Mama Mural

When Mama saw your mural
She was filled
With love and joy and radiance divine
Genetic recognition shone
Her smiling eyes in every line.

When Mama saw your mural
She was proud
So proud of your great artistry
Your wondrous leadership within
A vibrant collectivity.

When Mama saw your mural
How she laughed
Burst into laughter just to see
Her dreams transformed, made real at last
Reach out to all humanity.

When Mama saw your mural
Yes, she cried
To see the overarching beauty there
Bright through the tears in vision glow
Rainbow of womanspirit everywhere.

Then Mama hugged and kissed you
You both felt many stories tall
"Maestrapeace,"
She whispered in your ear,
Then merged with all the women on the wall.

Note: Truly a "Maestrapeace," the mural of this name shines
forth from the Women's Building on 18th Street in San
Francisco. My sister Miranda, creator of murals around the
world, played a primary role in this herstoric mural. Of
course, she would be the first to say that the other six great
muralists, the calligrapher, and many volunteers truly
breathed collective life into this monumental work. Her life
as an artist has made manifest the dreams of my mother, also
an artist, while reflecting her own powerful personality and
revolutionary dedication to art as a way to celebrate life,
involve and inspire people of the community, spark social
change, and vision freedom and equality. Miranda is hereby
nominated for one of those MacArthur "genius" awards, so
she can continue ever-beckoning mural projects without
financial woes. She would put this or any other grant to
wonderful use by creating more "maestrapeaces."

One More for Chris

(given with a large blue geode)

For our friendship
Brother-hood
And Love
All of which
Has been, is, and will always be
Multi-layered, beautiful,
And solid as a rock.

Anna on Stage

Anna on stage
So poised, so confident,
Having such a good time
Great, sure dancing
Joyous rapt involvement
Singing, acting
Putting it all together
In wonderful ways:
Comic role in "You Can't Take It With You"
Lots of roles in Evita
New productions pending
Sharing the lead in "City of Angels"
Whirlwind of rehearsals
Anna on stage
Anna blossoming
Anna coming into her own
A great young woman
Beautiful and talented
Daughter shining on stage
So great to see
Her loving it so much
So great to see
Anna on stage.

On Turning 50

At 50 this is all I know
Water helps the plants to grow
Minerals and sunlight's glow
At 50 this is all I know.

Love the way that children say
They're "turning" a new age
Like autumn leaf or circling wheel
Or turning the next page.

I'm thankful for each day of grace
Amidst this oft-times maddening pace
And hope, before I end the race,
My poems will find a rightful place.

On turning fifty this I know
Praise helps all living things to grow
Tender care and lovelight's glow
At 50 this is all I know.

Elapsing of half century
In fingersnap of time
Sorrow, pain, and happiness
Less reason and more rhyme.

Great cycle of our nights and days
Gift me the might to turn a phrase
To wind life's vast and complex maze
Seek clarity amidst the haze.

On turning fifty this I know
Change can happen fast or slow
Stream may dry or overflow
At 50 this is all I know.

To all of you my cup I raise
Who've been there when I start to fade
Been open to my moon's next phase
Supported me in countless ways.

To all of you these lines are sent
In thankfulness and testament
Links of loving most of all
As autumn leaves begin to fall.

At 50 this is all I know
Water helps the plants to grow
Minerals and sunlight's glow
At 50 this is all I know.

Acid Rain Limericks

There once was an oxide named NO_x
Who, along with another called SO_x,
Unleashed acid rain,
As this guide will explain,
Causing eco-illogical shocks.

From smokestacks and auto exhaust
Exacting a terrible cost
Acid rain's killing lakes
Do we have what it takes—
To make certain that no more get lost?

The tough problems posed by pollution
Are crying out loud for solution
To bring NO_x and SO_x down
Let us meet in our town
For we each have a key contribution.

Tessellation Jingle

Build tessellations, bit by bit,
Repeating patterns, perfect fit,
Like checkerboards or bathroom tiles—
Make patterns stretch for miles and miles.
Remember: There can be no gap;
All shapes must fit, not overlap.

Note: The poems on pages 260–270, except for the two top verses on page 267, have appeared in publications of the Great Explorations in Math and Science (GEMS) program, copyright by The Regents of the University of California. I've been really gratified that so many teachers have told me they like one poem or another—and in some cases students have dramatized them—like the Global Warming limericks. One Midwest summer camp put a verse of the Time and the River poem on its T-shirts. Most of all I enjoy writing them!

Ode to the Earthworm

A pause to thank this worm of earth
Through which life's nutrients come to birth
The butt of many jokes and hurt
Tunneler in tons of dirt
The leaves that fall from autumn trees
Ingested are by worms like these
Mixed in the soil, so new plants thrive
Earthworm's labor keeps people alive
Small pinkish thing of so much worth
We thank you gently worm of earth.

Penguin Deluxe

Penguin deluxe
Bird in a tux
Elegant, debonair
Birds of a feather
Who *do* flock together
But never take to the air.

The Sun is a Star

Our teacher told us
The Sun is a star
The closest to us
But still pretty far
It's lucky for us
When nighttime is done
That it knows how to turn
Into a Sun!

Stability

Within this wondrous world of change
As atoms clash and re-arrange
There yet remains some constancy
The anchor of stability.

Experiments one lab refines
Can be performed time after time
If variables are well-controlled
The same results are sure to hold.

A chemical reaction's change
Is also only fair exchange
Though liquid may turn into gas
There's no change in the total mass.

Rock at bottom of a hill
Gravity keeps it there still
In every system balance comes
When reaching equilibriums.

In all these ways and many more
Stability's like solid floor
A centered place, a balanced range,
Amidst the ocean roar of change.

On Sandy Shores
(with all due apologies to William Wordsworth)

On sandy shores
On sandy shores
That's where I love to roam
On sandy shores
Life of all kinds
Makes its home sweet home.

On sandy shores
The habitats
Tell many different stories
On sandy shores
The tidepools teem
With life in all its glories.

Why does the sand crab move that way?
Why did the tide just slide away?
Why do those birds have such big bills?
Why do there have to be oil spills?
Is seaweed really good for you?
Are sharks afraid of humans too?

All this and more
My mind explores
When inward eye
Sees sandy shores—
And then my heart with pleasure flows
To feel the sand between my toes.

Of Time and the River

I.

How to imagine
The span of time
The erosion of earth
In stone called lime
The cutting of granite
Of soil or sand
Water, ice, wind
Their carving hand.

How to imagine
Time's vast flow
The dimmer it seems
The longer ago
And all that has happened
With humans on scene
Is scarcely a blip
On time's vast stream.

The raising of mountains
Earthquake, uplift
Glaciers scoop basins
Continents shift
Some changes are massive
Sudden and strong
Others take eons
Longer than long.

Vainly we seek
For the best metaphor
To open up time's
Immemorial door
To clearly explain
Such incredible scope
Billions of knots
On Earth's counting rope.

Imagine a flower
With petals unfurled
A beautiful rose
As big as the world
Each layer of petals
One million years old
Yet still there would be
Countless ages untold.

Imagine a valley
Winding and deep
Cut by a river
As we wake and sleep
Droplet by droplet
Inches to feet
Dried by the sun
Fed by the sleet.

Of time and the river
Great writers speak
Observing the ripples
On stream or creek
Caught, like us all,
In the great mystery
As time like a river
Flows to the sea.

II.
Time is a river
That flows to the sea
Carving the earth
Quite gradually

Time is a river
Flood on the rise
Changing the land
Before our eyes

Time is a river
An instant aware
Of leaping trout
Poised in air

Time is a river
Whose currents have seen
Dinosaur babies
Paddlewheel steam

Time is a river
It's all in the flow
Past, present, future,
Where does time go?

Time is a poem
Rhythm and rhyme
Time is a river
And rivers take time.

Planetary Verses

I love the planets in all their splendor
They whirl elliptical in Milky Way
The Sun, resplendent at their center,
Gives us heat energy, lights up our day.

Mercury, the smallest and the closest to the Sun
Mercury, the god, of course, was the fastest one.

Venus, love goddess, shrouded in mist
Beneath evening star, many lips have been kissed.

Earth—wondrous mother of life itself
From molten core to continental shelf.

Mars, named for the god of war,
Red rusty surface, with iron at core.

The prize to Jupiter for immensity
Red Spot a storm of great intensity.

Wondrous amazement the sight of Saturn brings,
Famous for its necklace of at least 10,000 rings!

Neptune with his trident, ruler of the sea—
The planet is a cold one, way too cold for you or me.

Uranus's axis, near-horizontal, spins
Fifteen moons, eleven rings, very rapid winds.

Pluto of the Underworld, sits upon his throne.
Rocky icy outpost on the edge of the unknown.

They rotate and revolve, spinning tops through space,
Orbit in a spiral dance of such amazing grace.

I love the planets in all their splendor
They whirl elliptical in Milky Way
The Sun, resplendent at their center
Gives us heat energy, lights up our day.

Note: Since the above was for a teacher/student publication I couldn't use the best one, about Uranus.

Uranus was the butt of jokes, back in the olden days,
They changed pronunciation, but it happens anyways!

Brief Ode to Glenn

Tall and gangly
He'd come down to
My cubicle
To chat about
Our next column
In the *GEMS Network News.*

Glenn, beaming
At the periodic table
Birthday cake
Featuring seaborgium—
He wears his fame
Like an old favorite sweater.

Note: As part of my work at Lawrence Hall of Science, a sort of
friendship/collaboration developed between me and Glenn
Seaborg, the Nobel Laureate whose team "discovered"
plutonium. He headed the Atomic Energy Commission under
four U.S. Presidents, and helped engineer the nuclear test-ban
treaty. To his credit, he was also one of the young scientists who
opposed Truman's genocidal dropping of the atomic bomb,
arguing for a demonstration on an uninhabited island so the
Japanese brass could witness its power. Of course, he and I did
not see eye to eye on many things, but we collaborated/ghost
wrote successfully on many columns about science education. He
was a unique chemical mixture of homespun friendliness,
monumental egotism, and political savvy. At one science
teacher's convention he and his wife Helen (the great woman
behind the man) regaled us with stories of their courtship and
marriage. On hand was a periodic table birthday cake celebrating
the naming of the transuranium element seaborgium after him.
I recited these limericks:

> There was a Nobelist of men
> Whose birthday has come round again
> How proved he so able
> At the periodic table?
> Element'ry my dear, chuckled Glenn.

> Cake candles glimmer in flame
> To light up some measure of fame
> In terms of a gift
> It gives quite a lift
> When an element takes on your name!

The Plates by Edgar Allan Bergman

Hear the pounding of the plates—
   Massive plates
What a crust of constant change their throbbing thrum
relates
   How they thunder, thunder, thunder
    In the deep recess of soil
   While hot magmas rush asunder
   And the heavens glare in wonder
    As all slowly comes to boil
    Keeping time, time, time
    In a geologic rhyme
To the tectonabulation that so loudly emanates
   From the plates, plates, plates, plates
    Plates, plates, plates—
From the thunder and the wonder of the plates.

Hear the great tectonic plates
   Moving plates!
What a vast cacophony their clashing stimulates
Through the day and through the night
How they shift with main and might
And the molten mantle burns
Plates collide
What a thrum of twist and turn
Homes and hearts begin to shake, stomachs churn
In wild ride
Oh, from grinding plates it grates
What a rush of energy its labor liberates!
How it breaks
How it cakes
As the ore-filled oven bakes
Of the power that it makes
To the turning and the churning
Of the plates, plates, plates, plates
Plates, plates, plates
The burning and the churning of the plates.

See the ridged volcanic plates
   Magma gates
What a story of eruption, now, their turbulency states!

In the startled eye of sight
How we roar out our delight
Too incredible to speak
We can only shriek. shriek, shriek
With deep fright
In a clamorous explosion made of molten rock on fire
In a mad expostulation of a fierce frantic fire
Leaping higher, higher, higher
With a desperate desire
Till unfurrowed faults do sever
Now—now to flow forever
By the side of cratered moon.
O the plates, plates, plates
What a tale their twist relates
       Of great mass!
How they clang and clash and roar!
What a lava they outpour
From the cauldron of the palpitating gas!
Yet the people fully know
By the banging,
And the clanging
How the dangers ebb and flow
Yet the sound distinct berates
In the jangling
And the wrangling
How the danger always waits
By the drifting and the shifting in the angle of the plates—
Of the plates—
Of the plates, plates, plates, plates,
       Plates, plates, plates
In the clamor and the clangor of the plates!
Hear the rolling of the plates—
       Rugged Plates!
What a world of awesome might their majesty inflates!
       In the violence of the night
       How we quiver with affright
At the geologic menace of their tone!
For every sound that floats
From the quartz within their throats
  Is a groan.
And the people—ah, the people—
They that dwell up in the steeple,
       All Alone

And who, toiling, toiling, toiling
In excited multi-tone
Feel a glory in so rolling
　On the human heart a stone
They are neither sea nor shore
They are neither crust nor core
They are Coals
Mother Earth's hot brimming bowls
And she rolls, rolls, rolls
　Rolls
An anthem from the plates!
And her heaving breast inflates
With the pounding of the plates
And she dances and creates
Keeping time, time, time
In a geologic rhyme
To the pounding of the plates
Of the plates
Keeping time time time
In a geologic rhyme
To the sliding of the plates
Of the plates, plates, plates—
To the gliding of the plates
Keeping time, time, time
As she swells, swells, swells,
In a true tectonic rhyme
To the churning of the plates
Of the plates, plates, plates
To the turning of the plates
Of the plates, plates, plates, plates—
Plates, plates, plates—
To the shaking and the quaking of the plates.

-The End-

Fifty Lines for Fifty-Year-Olds

Half century may seem substantial time
To those of us who have that measure grown
Yet ponder centuries that course our blood
Genetic memories of sea and stone
Reflect upon the ages cells have known
Footsteps of geologic habitat
On this green whirling pea that's round—
Though once thought flat.

The shifting of tectonic plates
Stew of elements within the Earth
The moment when a lightning bolt
Sent one cell dancing into birth
Yes, in our very blood throbs yet
A prehistoric rhythmic chant
Eons of adaptation cast their net
Ocean source of animal and plant

Did clever dinosaurs evolve to birds?
Who were first creatures to use words?
Music to Neanderthals was known
As witness unearthed flute of bone
Cro-Magnon beings rise then fall
Homo sapiens comes in from the rain
Inside us Lucy, mother of us all
Strides miles across the Serengheti plain.

Fire tamed, a candle in the night,
Murals in the caverns of Lascaux
Matriarchy dances in moonlight—
Inside our cells such things we know
Of eras past, we know the parts,
Of eye for eye and tooth for tooth
Witches burned for healing arts
Rebels crucified for speaking truth.

War famine pestilence slash all
The agonies of cruelty's blade
Yet rising as a clarion call
The difference that some have made.
Social movements roll high tide
Migrations like vast rivers trace
Open in deltas spreading wide
To ocean of our rainbow race.

Return us now, on this a day of birth
To ancient truths inside the Earth
To evolution's family tree
To lava's ancient memory
Though only one-half-century old
We hold the greatest story told
Millions of years within us found—
Time lets nobody turn it round.

Within this context then for birthday song
A mere half century seems not so long!

Working Hands (after Brecht)

Who raised the wonders of all lands?
For Pyramids who hauled the stone?
All were made by working hands
Not by Pharoah on his throne.

So heed the writing on the walls
And sing the freedom song
When something rises, something falls,
Hands that work grow strong.

The future is a child in birth
The labor has been long
To build a just and peaceful earth
Hands that work grow strong.

Great Mother Matriarch

Meridel—
Thinking of you tonight:

Great Mother Matriarch
Just like a Tree
Standing by the water
We shall not be moved

Your steady strength
Celebrates struggle
Wordwisdom
Harvest of your long Life
Work destined to extend

For eons onward toward
Earthrises of Freedom
Circular, harmonious, whole,
Changeable as Moon phases

Onward Equality
Grown into daily reality
Rooted in Indigenous soil
Just like a Tree

Standing by the water
Blossoming your name.

Children Like Plants

for Karen and Morgan   April 2, 1995

Children like plants
Need nutrients so
Bodies and branches
Strengthen and grow
Tended with tenderness
Nurtured with care
Tiny fingers that grip
Little booties to wear
Beautiful baby leaps into light
Cuddled and cradled
To make things all right
Tended with tenderness
Nurtured with care
Beginning to focus,
Becoming aware
Of Karen and Morgan
Mama and dad
They'll be two of the best
That a child ever had
And though it's not easy
And hurdles abound
I can't help but be sure
Happiness will resound
Will sing in the branches
Like birds on the wing
In a chorus of caring
Open-throated as spring
Walk heavy as wheat stalk
Bending toward earth
Let life swell downward
Vase and vessel of birth
Let child knock against you
In stretch, arch, and spin
Rise like a dolphin
On seas deep within

Tended with tenderness
Nurtured with care
Genetic uniqueness
That all of us share
Diversity's darling
Wondrous and wild
Miraculous light
In the eyes of a child
Miraculous might
In a mother's fierce love
Light beaming down
From her eyes high above
Lullaby liltings
Of fatherhood's song
To welcome dear baby
Robust and strong
For children like plants
Need nutrients so
Bodies and branches
Can strengthen and grow
Each day a blossoming
Fragrant and fair
Smooth as new skin
Or soft sprouting hair
Children like plants
Push toward the light
Flowering spirits
Who dance in delight
Tended with tenderness
Nurtured with care
Children like plants
Who give us our air.

Post-Election November 9, 1994

weather blusters
wilson sputters
anti-immigrant invective
gains the racist day

weather blusters
good hearts flutter
poet emma lazarus
rolls over in her grave

weather blusters
clinton mutters
bipartisan malarkey
is the chatter of the day

weather blusters
close the shutters
"big government's" the reason
for society's decay

weather blusters
in the gutters
health coverage for all is not
the patriotic way

weather blusters
as crop dusters
poison babies of farmworkers
agribusiness holding sway

weather blusters
union busters
strikers pound the pavements
seeking raises long-delayed

weather blusters
tv sputters
basic bread and butter
shrinks from day to day

weather blusters
no one musters
unifying vision
of more equitable way

will weather ever clear
will bluster ever cease
will we learn respect
will we ever live in peace?

judging from this sad election
the answer would be "no"
this cancerous infection
just seems to grow and grow

about the only ray
of sunlight on the street
is rent control in berkeley
and ollie north's defeat

perhaps there's other plus-es
other local issues won
but in general the outcome's
more than enough to stun

the hardiest of optimists
those with the longest view
i ask you, sisters, brothers
what are we gonna do?

who will proclaim new vision
with clarity and care
who will truly organize
to help us head somewhere

who will face confusion
and overcome despair
who will sing again my friends
of freedom in the air

i do not know the answers
but this much I do know
it will take many voices
to make real chorus grow

nor can i claim with certainty
that victory will come
but I know that in the trying
when all is said and done

there is a certain meaning
a dignity and grace
that comes with daily struggle
on behalf of human race

so whether don Quixote,
or better Rosa Parks
the light that dawns in children's eyes
those precious learning sparks

are nurtured by our efforts
to build better ways between
our own internal psyches
and the complex social scene

the worth is in the doing
the lessons in the task
only in the process
are leading questions asked

only in the doing
will the grapes of wrath be squeezed
into the wine of wisdom
the fruits of freedom seized

only in the doing
will our children's children see
there were some among us
who envisioned liberty.

A Few Millennial Appreciations

'Ere this millennium slips away
There's something I've just got to say:

There were people in this century
Whose examples set the stage
They deserve to be remembered.
As time proceeds to turn the page.

I do not speak of Presidents
Nor stars of field or screen
The glitterati of the press
Are not the people who I mean.

Some gained great measure of respect
Attained some modicum of fame
But many passed unheralded
Unknown to most by deed or name.

Most have heard of Martin King
And Malcolm's meaning grows each day
Yet Jacksons, George and Jonathan,
Their martyrdom stays locked away.

The prisoners at Attica
Who rose rebellious unified
Students—Kent and Jackson State
All other protestors who died.

Go back further and we find
Helen Keller, who was not blind
To freedom—a strong socialist
Something that the textbooks missed!

Dubois and Robeson
Millions reached
Debs, Gurley Flynn,
Class lessons teach

In every land
I know we'd find
Those who stood
And spoke their mind.

Those who strove for freedom's share
Who truly treasured human worth
In the midst of war and greed
Revolutions shook the earth

Every grandmother and child
Who harbored freedom in their hearts
All cultural contributors
Who etched equality in arts.

Longshore workers on the docks
Who took a distant people's side
Refused to work with ships blood-soaked
By Pinochet or apartheid.

Every single person who
Rose high tide on freedom's shore
Defied the might of Empire
Forced an end to unjust war.

So many more, the list goes on
Their hearts to humankind they gave
Joined together, each unique,
Many millions in a wave.

For each of them these lines of praise
My gift to them this simple phrase:
Though night is long before the dawn
The game may yet go to the pawn!

Sonnet for Miranda   April 1996

The tempests of the human heart can rage
Can sometimes sorely strain our mortal frames
Complex emotions fill each turning page
Of book of life that has so many names.
Sweet sister dear whichever paths we've trod
Where joy and pain beat hearts upon a drum
I pledge upon the sacred goddess sod
In ways we can't foresee "our day will come."

Great person and great artist whom thou art—
That's gospel truth although you wrestle doubt,
Believe it, yes believe, deep in your heart,
That tempest-tossed will find its own way out.

Whatever ways you reach your next plateau
You have my love and love is all I know.

Mother's Day 1997

Whirl of life and death
Grand forks of floods
Anguish out of Africa
Palestinian persistence.

Unfinished poem
Crossing the century
Photo of my mother
On the shore

Waving in the days
Before her death.

For Arch Williams   June 1996

It was a cold windy night when Archie died
Also Ella Fitzgerald was ushered inside
And Max Mandel, 102, bid goodbye to all of us too:

For Archie For Archie
Who faced the day
Who enlightened our walls
With spirit so gay
Who passed on to children
Great art and its power
Nurtured the murals
That everywhere flower
On fences, in alleys,
Down schoolway halls
For Archie For Archie
Who enlightened our walls.

For Archie For Archie
Who encouraged and taught
Visioned the future
So soulfully sought
Whose work will inspire
Brush strokes of tomorrow:
Where courage and dignity
Shine through the sorrow.

His murals reflections
Of the person inside
Who shone like an angel
With us did reside
Both gentle and strong
Like curve of an arch
Holding up spirits
On our long march
To justice and peace
For beauty and love
Painted in rainbows
Arching above
His spirit is rising
Where liberty calls
For Archie For Archie
Who enlightened our walls.

For Archie For Archie
Who lives on in us all.

For Bernie—on his 70th (with Love from "Junior")

Improvising uncle
Has a special bop to be
Always has his zest for life
Enlightened nephew me
Scat to raise the rafters
Plenty of pizazz
Energy abundant
Laughs and all that jazz
Syncopated rhythm
Sophisticated swing
Wild creative projects
While the big bands sing
Giant wooden puzzles
Recycled beasts of box
Joie de vivre unending
Beat to knock off socks
Improvising uncle
Has a special bop to be
All my love wails to him
As he swings to seventy!

Five Haikus (November 1997)

Martin and Barbara
Baritone and alto
Both looking so good!

Big Apple
Meets San Francisco—
Manhattan Opera in the flesh!

Music and murals
Poems and puns
Create works of lasting value!

Her penknife carves
Along the winding weave of wood
So time sculpts our lives!

Open-throat song
Crescendo of emotion
Long live the human voice!

For Frank and Karen   10/30/97

House of two artists
Nestled in river embrace
Mountain ocean forest
Redwood madrone alder
Points of light and pigment
Paintings flow Eel River
Into Sea of Creativity
Home of two painters
Studios of lucent clarity
Nestled in river embrace.

Note: Frank Cierciorka and Karen Horne dwell in rustic
beauty and artistic splendor. She is a nationally esteemed
watercolorist whose paintings boggle the mind in their
larger-than-life reality. He is an artist for all seasons, beauti-
ful land and oceanscapes, nudes, cartoons, poster art, and
lots more, including the famous fist icon of the 1960s (see
page 294).

On That Bridge

Today
I'm here at work
But O my feet
March on that bridge
I couldn't go
But O my soul
Sings on that bridge!

August 28, 1997
Jesse Jackson leads march against Proposition 209
across the Golden Gate Bridge.

Thinking Continually of Mario—
Who Was Truly Great

I think continually of Mario
Mario in mid-speech
Thinking out loud with us
Seeming to be speaking
To each person's spirit
Profoundly democratic
Eloquent, articulate,
Our Demosthenes who
Once stammered badly
But in Free Speech discourse
Spun uniquely compelling
Webs of logic and passion
Many-sided, dialectical
Truthful and sincere
Complex and coherent
Modest and magnificent.

When he spoke to the
Assembled multitudes
Electrons vibrated
With the right to rebel
Going to the root of things
Calling out the score
Empowering the mass of us
Humanity at core.

Prophetic words of beauty
Vision of a place
Where all will be respected
Not judged upon their face
Where all will have a chance
To learn, to grow, to teach,
And all will have a right
To celebrate free speech.

Mario Savio will live on
His life will have great reach
I think continually of Mario
Mario in mid-speech.

Teach brother teach!

Mario to Meridel: A Meditation

From Mario to Meridel
Death rolls inexorable
Each a voice of generation.

From Meridel to Mario
Winter devours
The great circle spirals.

Corn mother matriarch
Whose art and struggle
Span the century
Whose spirit
Lives forever in
The kernel of rebellion.

Lean brother prophet
Whose speeches
Sang freedom songs
Whose spirit
Sprouts forever from
The seed of justice.

From Meridel to Mario
Root of resistance
Salute to Spring.

From Mario to Meridel
Deep inspiration
Moving us onward.

Note: Mario Savio and Meridel Le Sueur were great souls among us, rooted in the soil of the people. Mario, taken at the tender age of 53, was, in the words of José Marti, an *hombre sincero*, a truthful man, whose eloquence, logic, and love of justice harmonized with compassion, modesty, and passionate belief in democracy. Meridel died on November 14, 1996 at the age of 96. She wrote acclaimed proletarian short stories in the 1930s, lasting children's books in the 1950s, and a vast array of Revolutionary, Feminist, Indigenous, and Global Village poetry and experimental works. Famous in Minnesota and treasured by writers worldwide she encouraged, and by a tribal extended family of numerous grandchildren, great-grandchildren, and great-great grandchildren, Meridel's wide-ranging work has only just begun to attain the recognition it deserves. Days before she died she and the collective she worked with, Midwest Villages and Voices, published *Irene*, the writings of Meridel's friend Irene Paull. a dedicated poet and social activist who lived in San Francisco for many years.

Frère Allen

April 1997

"The beautiful souls are those that are universal, open, and ready for all things."

- Michel de Montaigne

Three verses for Allen Ginsberg, in his own
great spirit of rhyme and play and audience participation.
to be sung to the tune of "Frère Jacques."

Allen Ginsberg
Allen Ginsberg
Has passed on
Has passed on
Peaceful prophet poet
Find a seed and sow it
He's not gone
He's not gone.

Allen Ginsberg
Allen Ginsberg
Buddhist Jew
Buddhist Jew
Ringing in the spirit
Everyone can hear it
He rang true
He rang true.

Allen Ginsberg
Allen Ginsberg
Good gay seer
Good gay seer
Rage against the warlord
Singing out the life chord
He's still here
He's still here!

Note: This poem won an "Honorable Mention" in a local newspaper's (The *San Francisco Bay Guardian*) poetry contest. Does this make me a "prizewinning poet!?" If so, it is thanks to the great Ginsberg!

Robert Williams

And before I'd be a slave
I'd be buried in my grave
Take my place with those who fought to be free...

I knew Robert Williams in China
His reputation preceded him:
Militant author of *Negroes with Guns*
NAACP leader charged with kidnapping
For protecting some whites amidst racial turmoil
Went first to Cuba
Sent out fiery *Crusader* newsletter
Broadcast Radio Free Dixie
Then to Africa and China
Where I first met him in Peking
With Mabel and his two sons
He had a Robeson dignity
A Malcolm intensity and his own
Brilliant mind and monumental power
Highly disciplined and well-organized.
I remember at that time
He ate just one meal a day
Got up to a huge breakfast.

Later I saw him back in the States
In the company of Vicki Garvin and my father
Always deeply impressed
By the forward-moving power of that man.
He'd faced the Klan demons
Taken freedom crusade around the world
Then came back, vindicated himself
Settled up North
Made many contributions
To the battle against heroin in Detroit
His heart with his people
Struggling to save the children
In the last years of his life
Working on his autobiography.

Robert Williams stands
In leadership pantheon
With Medgar and Malcolm
Harriet and Frederick
Dubois and Fannie Lou
Towering through the century.
Oh, Freedom over me!
Takes his place
With those who fought to be free.

Different Then

I was somewhat different then
I'm not sure who and not sure when
I changed into the self I am
I know that I was strong and clear
And all the things that I held dear
I still avow and would defend
Yet I was someone different then
I know it was the times as well
Surging tide wove wondrous spell
Yet there are those who kept their aim
Who were not swallowed in the game
Who still are out there, fists upraised
That's who my lines most seek to praise.

Silly Sonnet on Poetic Ambition

One decent sonnet's all this poet asks
No novel, great American or not,
No Broadway play or operatic masque—
Just fourteen lines is all the hope I've got!

Will Shakespeare brought the sonnet to a place
No other soul has ever wandered near
He somehow knew that years would not erase
Ideas and images he held so dear.

Love is the soil where sonnets stake their claim
But shining nuggets few and far between
Though Browning counts her ways to lasting fame
Most other efforts languish sight unseen.

One sonnet I continue to pursue,
But this ain't it—and that for sure is true!

> *Optional last line:*
> But this ain't it—that sure as shit is true!

KPFA Limericks

A Pacifica Board chair named Berry
Mary Frances, much power did carry
She did wield her Chadwick
Like proverbial big stick
In a manner both brutal and scary.

Community that is the key
Control should reside locally
Using CPB sword
They ripped off local board
To take power illegally.

Sawaya, then Bensky, were gone
Soon Osman's great program spat on
Name of next show to go
Proved prophetic you know
Flashpoints off and the battle was on!

YES the people en masse did awake
That's our station, they said, you can't take
We will here make our stand
On this place on wave band
Free speech we can never forsake.

If some enemy had made a plan
To murder Mumia, oh man,
Would they, on the way there
Take over our air—
Could that be why this hit the fan?

Conspiracy theories aside
Chadberry has looted and lied
All armed guards must cease
Disturbing the peace
And their Board ops must be swept aside!

It's a constant struggle that's true
Freedom, and all we must do
To protect and defend
Best tidings we send
To Elsa and Mama and Lew.

And saludos to comrade Mandel
And too many others to tell
The 95 purge
Was one source of this scourge
Those wounds must be treated as well.

Loco, Spearhead, and Utah did sing
Joan's voice with beauty did ring
In days packed with passion
The people did fashion
A program that truly took wing.

Mario's spirit is here
Expressing all we hold dear
The power of truth
The flower of youth
Equality coming in clear.

Judi Bari was way out ahead
Saw how Foundation misled
Spoke out before dying
To the end ever-trying
To save sacred woods we call red.

Yes, it's time for a radical change
New programs of power and range
Rainbows of all races
Young and old faces
Engaged in an open exchange.

Social justice the heart of the matter
Not polluting the air with more chatter
An eclectic air sound
Breaking cultural ground
Not helping consultants grow fatter!

And oh how the battle does grow
Chadwick and Berry must go
Raise democracy's cup
Rebuild from ground up
We've still got a long road to hoe.

I will sing out these lines on that day
When once more with pride we can say
This is our freedom station
We've won its liberation
Let's celebrate that every day!

I Sing the Radio Eclectic
or Democracy—When?

For Elsa Knight Thompson, Mama O'Shea, Samori Marksman,
Mumia Abu Jamal, Kwame Turé, Leonard Peltier, and all others
who, with Malcolm, have understood the "power of truth,"
and with all due apologies to Walt Whitman and Allen Ginsberg.

I sing the radio eclectic—the varied programs I hear
Chant essence of community broadcast
Dynamic link between listener and programmer
Stand with growing thousands demanding return

Of Sawaya, Bensky, Osman, Bernstein, and free speech.
Declare "gag rule" unconstitutional.
Affirm people's air to be open, analytical, questioning,
Curious, daring, profoundly democratic.

Further declare the fix has been in for years
No money comes without strings
Strategic plan hatched by earlier misleaders
The purge of 95 allowed to happen with little protest.

And yes, there's always need for change
But in order to better pursue truth and justice
Not to fit into some marketing consultant's
Auditron-driven image of professional sound

Is this the same Pacifica that played a significant role
In spread of civil rights movement?
Birth of student movement
Abolition of House UnAmerican Activities Committee?

The same Pacifica that broadcast Robeson?
Lorraine Hansberry, James Baldwin, Allen Ginsberg?
Gloried in off-beat cultural exploration
Contributed to U.S. defeat in Vietnam?

See how Pacifica, an independent voice
Has been befouled by CPB funds—
Since when can a federal official
Became Chair of its Board of Directors?

Communities awaken but at first
Programming continues in surreal fashion
As armed guards patrol the airwaves
Then a flashpoint moment erupts

Station is a locked down prison
Chain and lock across the door
That once meant open access
Demonstrations swell

Pacifica, maneuvered to the right
Will you be shipwrecked by corporate greed
Or can we unite, as in courageous stories you have told
To build new foundation from ashes of old?

For nothing is stronger than the power of truth.
Great divides can be crossed.
We are all living on Indian time
And freedom *is* a constant struggle.

6/24/99

Note: Freedom Is A Constant Struggle was the name of the weekly radio show on KPFA produced by many people, including Barbara Lubinski, Heber Dreher, Emilano Eccheverria, Nina Serrano, Kiilu Nyasha, and myself. It was continuation of earlier programs produced by Claude Marks, Nancy Barrett, myself, and others, and named The Midnight Flash, The Real Dragon, and Nothing Is More Precious Than...Living on Indian Time was a program on KPFA. Freedom is A Constant Struggle and Living on Indian Time were among many programs and programmers taken off the air in 1995, during what some described as a political purge. The recordings of our programs were saved over the years, and make up an important part of The Freedom Archives (see inside back cover for more information).

For Kwame Turé
(to the tune of Freight Train)

Stokely Stokely
Gone so fast
Stokely Stokely
Life went past
We'll be singin'
Freedom song
As Kwame passes on

Kwame Turé that's his name
Early on he won great fame
Even though he now is gone
In our struggle he lives on.

Note: I knew Kwame Turé very slightly, respected him greatly, heard him as the dynamic charismatic speaker who, as Stokely Carmichael, was one of the top leaders of the Student Non-Violent Coordinating Committee (SNCC). Knew of a brief Black Panther alliance, heard of his marriage to Miriam Makeba and its end, and that his politics had developed in a Pan-African socialist direction. I was very saddened on hearing he had cancer. Through Vicki Garvin I sent him some books he needed on the African-American liberation struggle because he was still studying and struggling during the last year of his life. He lives on!

Millennial Sonnet

Let arbitrary notch in time be damned
The meaning of the moment's not in this
Though media may be milleni-crammed
Be not distracted by their howling hiss
A global crisis swirls around us friends
Life and the planet in the balance scales
As capital pursues its selfish ends
And ethics yields to purchases and sales
Rights of the child United Nations passed
Yet witness homeless children everywhere
How long my friends will this unfreedom last
Amidst razed redwoods and polluted air
Destruction or survival—that's the choice
For global social justice raise your voice!

Fist of Resistance (for Claude's 50th)

Fist of resistance
Long may it rise
Be it Sacco's, Vanzetti's
Julia Butterfly's

Rosa's or Malcolm's
Nelson's or Ho's
Masses in motion
Wherever fist goes

In Vieques or Timor
On streets of Seattle
Inside prison walls
Calling to battle

Indigenous wisdom
Courage of youth
Carry us forward
Shout out the truth

Fist of resistance
To counter their lies
As century passes
May fist symbolize

New spirit dawning
Strong energy surge
Que viva la causa
New voices emerge

A powerful drawing
From year '65
Tells us that struggle
Keeps freedom alive.

Ode to a Knee

Ode to a knee
That knob of much use
That complex mechanical
Angle obtuse; that
Lever, that hinge,
That pivotal point
Ode to the knee
That remarkable joint.
(Though contoured in cartilage,
Under that shell
Knee tissue's vulnerable
Painful as hell.)

Taken for granted
These bony plateaus
Are often derided
In bowlegged pose,
But when they are aching
Or out of commission
When they can't bend
Or hurt like the dickens
Then the truth becomes clear
Consciousness grows—
Knees do great deeds
Poised over our toes.

Ode to a knee
Muscles delicate, deft
Staunch support on the right
Likewise on the left
Day in and day out
Knees hold up our heft.

Felix, these lines are written for you
Just a few lines long overdue
Penned shortly thereafter
Eclipse of the moon
Hope that your knee
Gets better real soon!

Message to Geronimo   June 15, 1997
(Closing quotation courtesy of Ho Chi Minh)

George invoked this creature
Before they shot him down
"Big Black" and all of Attica
Heard its awesome sound

Its fiery breath flared freedom
On Africa's vast shore
Inside apartheid dungeon
Mandela heard its roar

It's there to help Mumia
Comfort Leonard, lift the soul
Of all who are imprisoned
In pursuit of social goal

Geronimo, your freedom
Warms the cockles of its heart
Beating in the struggle
Where all must play their part

And for anyone who wonders
What this poem is all about—
"When the prison doors are opened,
The real dragon will fly out!"

Note: Just after his release, I sent this to Elmer "Geronimo" Ji Jaga
Pratt. Scores of Panthers and Black liberation fighters were killed
by police, hundreds were imprisoned, some remain unjustly behind
bars more than 30 years later. Full clemency for all these and other
political prisoners is long overdue. "Geronimo" was one of the
most capable and experienced Panther leaders. He was falsely
imprisoned for over 25 years—even though FBI surveillance
showed him in Oakland with other Panther leaders at the same
time Los Angeles police claimed he took part in a robbery-murder
incident. Years of persistent legal work led to his release, followed
by a big lawsuit for damages. It was a rare, victorious, happy
moment when he walked into the sunlight! The newspaper photos
of him hugging his grandkids did warm the heart!

March 17

Ma's date of death came and it went
I considered the day
Fairly well spent
The Ides of March
Slipped by this year
With just a modicum of fear
The date of her death came and went
I wish I could say
All that it meant
Wish I could say
To my two dears
How we have to make it
Through the tears
That I love them both
With all my heart
Well, maybe this poem is a start!

Keep the Spirit Alive in the Year '95!

An ode my friends to the year '95
To keep the spirit of spirits alive
No matter how the newt may turn
Or helms be held by those we spurn
An ode to caring cooperation
As mode of travel and destination
With open arms welcome immigrants in
Spread new roots to re-begin
Proclaim free health care a right of birth
Renew resources, reclaim the Earth
To outfox the frost, outlast the storm
Keep compassion's tiny fingers warm
To keep the spirit of spirits alive
An ode my friends to the year '95!

Sonnet for Anna at 21

When you were born how could we have foreseen
Your special spirit, grace, compassion, heart
In three times seven years upon the scene
You've honed your talents to a state of art

Did I say twenty-one? I can't believe
The years whirl by like West Side dancing feet
Today I wear my heart upon my sleeve
To wish that days ahead be full and sweet

Whatever ways your future paths may wind
Hold to a hand and you'll be halfway there
Sufficient strength, serenity you'll find,
With time to sing and share in open air.

Yes, twenty-one's an age change, that is true—
What does not change is all my love for you.

Another for Anna

Daughter dear I love you so
The light of moon, the soar of song,
I pray whichever paths you go
Love and luck will sing along.

Believing in yourself's the key
To pushing forward past the tide
Of culture's mediocrity
Take your rightful place beside

Singers, dancers, dreamers whose
Talent weaves a magic spell
Sing your soul and time will choose
Paths that lead to living well.

Madeleine

Large grey poodle
Sleeps, head forward,
Moping, patient,
Long-suffering
Madeleine
Sleeps
Dreaming of—
Elizabeth.

3 July

Lisa and me
In hot tub
Ginger barking
At the early
Fireworks
Red-grey clouds
Whirling winds
Whistle the bamboo
I sing the Billie song:
"Oh when I hear them say
There's better livin' let them go their way
To that new livin' I won't ever stray—
'Cause this is heaven to me...."
And for all the irony
I also know just what she means!

Sonnet for 1999

Cannot believe the years have Flown so fast
Cards of a centuRy dealt from the deck
RemEmbEring the people, places past
As next MillenniUm breathes down our neck !
These lines were writ upon a strange Machine
With powers unImagined years ago
That networked now constructs vAst brain unseen
Who can predict the dendrites it will grow?
Yet through it all let's bring things down to Earth
To nature's nut and seed and hands that hold
To joys of celebration, laughter, mirth
Worth so much more than all their hoarded gold.

These greetings come with warmth of human touch
To all fine folks we love so very much.

Note: It's not exactly a matter of reading between the lines,
but there is a message in some upper case letters (except any
that start a line) and I fervently urge it come to pass—along
with the freedom of all political prisoners!

Quick Poem: Computer Desktop

I have too many things on my desktop

Haven't even had time to
Drag them into appropriate folders.

This is a symbolic representation
Of how busy I am
Have reached the scattering level

Maybe the opening lines of this poem
Could become an au courant cliché
Since computers have become ubiquitous:

Dot.communists of the Earth, unite
You have nothing to lose but your domains—
And a world wide web to win!

Meanwhile, as Spring approaches,
My spirits definitely improve
Still this fact remains:

I have too many things on my desktop!

Moon over Rochdale Village

Brick high rises
World's largest co-op housing
When first built
Home of Mama Vicki
Who now speaks of
Nature and electricity
Energy everywhere
Who says—
"Nothing is static
Nothing is monolithic—
That's dialectics!"

Note: Rochdale Village is in Jamaica, Queens and this poem
records just a brief moment during a visit to Victoria Garvin.
Our Mama Vicki—a leading freedom fighter from the 1930s
on, a child of the Harlem Renaissance, the first African-
American woman to earn a graduate degree (in French
literature) from Smith, close friend and confidante of Paul
Robeson, W.E.B. DuBois, and many others. After helping
DuBois with the African Encyclopedia (in Ghana, where she
roomed for a time with Maya Angelou) and helping guide
Malcolm X on one of his Africa trips, she went on to teach
English in Shanghai for 10 years. In China she met my
father Leibel who, with me, had been teaching English in
Beijing (then Peking). Vicki and Leibel had a Red Guard
wedding! In the years after, first he and then she returned to
the United States, living and organizing politically in
Newark, New York City, and Chicago. Although they later
divorced, she kept in touch and we kept in touch. The love
grew and stayed strong. Also strong, Vicki's unremitting
commitment to African-American liberation and the world-
wide struggle for freedom, her energy, dedication—her
careful organization and powerful self-discipline—in all
these and in many other ways her example shines! We love
you Mama Vicki!

Betty's Blues (for Betty Shabazz)

Blues blues for Betty
Tragic bitter news
For her grandson Malcolm
Wild and wailing blues
Blues for her six daughters
For people struggling free
Blues for Betty people
Blues for you and me.

Blues inside that ballroom
More than thirty years ago
Shining Black prince murdered
Martyr's blood did flow
Eloquence and courage
The world that voice did reach
Blues inside that ballroom
Lord, that man could teach!

Blues blues for Betty
Tragic bitter news
For her grandson Malcolm
Wild and wailing blues
What could Malcolm know of Malcolm
Grandson know of leader's truth?
What is this system doing
To the blossom of our youth?

If I had the voice of Robeson
The lines of Langston Hughes
Then I might find the power
To truly sing these blues
With the wisdom of DuBois
The compassion of a King
Bessie, Billie, Dinah, Sarah
Then the Lord would bid me sing.

303

Sing to end this madness
Talk to people face to face
Sing of justice and of freedom
End oppression based on race
Give voice to end the terror
Silence poverty's shrill scream
Chant to shout the praises
Of the democratic dream.

Many came for tribute
Some solid all the way
But others were "come latelys"
Who never joined the fray
Still the people always know
Who truly pays their dues
Who gives their soul to struggle
Learns to sing the blues.

Blues blues for Betty
Body torn by flame
Millions keep on marching
Echoing her name
Betty was a shining star
Principles stayed pure
Blues for Betty people
Her example will endure.

Blues blues for Betty
Tragic bitter news
For her grandson Malcolm
Wild and wailing blues
Blues for her six daughters
For people struggling free
Blues for Betty people
Blues for you and me.

Recipe

Add a spoonful of Ginsberg
A measure of Wald
Some pinches of Nyro
Warm slowly, don't scald.

Season with Meridel
Fred Cody and Moe
Then sprinkle in spirits
Of others you know

Mix all together
Stir in a bowl
This recipe is
Food for the soul.

Note: The names here refer to poet Allen Ginsberg, Nobel
prizewinner and antiwar activist George Wald, singer Laura
Nyro, writer Meridel Le Sueur, and legendary Berkeley
bookstore owners Fred Cody and Moe Moscowitz, but there
are many more. Sprinkle in spirits of others you know.

Dementia

In shadows of dementia
The spirit still can shine
Creep out from the crevices
Of tangled brilliant mind
There—where there is laughter
Here—where there be tears
A sometime sparkle of the eyes
Can flash away the years!

Carnelian of Our Christmas Days
(given with a small agate to workmates)

Carnelian of our Christmas days
For you this earthen song of praise
Soulful solstice wishes sent
From every bed of sediment
Hewn Chanukahs of lasting light
Magma melt and muster might
Liquid lava rivers meet
In cooling oceans, fields of wheat
After harvest comes the cold
Carnelian let your tale be told.

Inspiring agate of my odes
In childhood on the dusty roads
I sought your crimson spirit glow
We seek it still, to learn and grow
As Earth recycles rocks and bones
Stories sing out from the stones.

Layers carol rock of ages
Turmoil all around us rages
To echo Shelley, will we find
With winter, Spring not far behind?
To echo Marley's anthem cry
Will we still make it if we try?

Shifting of tectonic plates
Rings of fire, furies, fates,
Chiselled paths of must-be-free
Carve their lustrous legacy
Harriet on freedom's road
Carpenter's son with heavy load
Nelson's jail cell, Frida's spirit,
Victor's song—I still can hear it,
Malcolm's parents, Ethel's poems,
Stories sing out from the stones.

Pressure rises through the crust
Mountains crumble into dust
Wild eruption, massive quake
Lithospheres of give and take
Gospel granite, spirit stones,
Sojourner Truth and Mother Jones.
Native wisdom, worldweb spin,
Echo lines of Ho Chi Minh:
Life's rock tumbler rolls its drum
To craft the gems we all become.

In deep volcanic crucible
Crystals form conducible
To geometric face and shape
Gemstones sculpted smooth as grape
Like the rock that David hurled
To knock Goliath from the world
To vanquish hunger, banish fear,
Of children all around the sphere
For you this rocky song of praise
Carnelian of our Christmas days.

On Mahealani's Death

I never thought I said good bye good enough
So here I'm saying it again & again
Good bye, Good bye, Good bye, Good bye
I send these good byes to you from Earth
To Heaven, to <u>you</u> a beautiful graceful
Angel floating in the sky.
Good bye, Good bye, Good bye & Good bye

I never thought I said I love you enough
So here I'm saying it again & again
I love you, I love you, I love you, I love you
I send this love from Earth
To Heaven, to <u>you</u> a beautiful graceful
Angel floating above
I do love, I do love, I do love

> by Caitlin Poema Simpson Bergman
> August, 1998
> Dedicated to my cousin, Mahealani

Note: Mahealani was the sweet, energetic, precious, and powerful daughter of my first cousin Robin's oldest son, Makeshda, and his partner Sage. After a long and valiant struggle against retinoblastoma, an eye cancer, Mahealani died not long after her third birthday. She was a miraculous presence in many lives, and most definitely in mine. This book is dedicated to my two daughters and to her. Her spirit sings in its best lines. I love this poem that Caitlin wrote to her.

Ending the Year 1998

Ending the year
In which
Mahaelani died
Rachel
Stokely too
Beginning the year
Before 2000
My mind casts back
Across the century
To Anne and Leibel
To Meridel
Morris and Doris
Sam and Molly
Just finished reading
Ex Libris by Anne Fadiman
Dedicated to her parents
I cry a bit and say out loud
That I never rose to
The level of literary achievement
To which I aspired
And might have attained.
Too soon to close the door on that
And yet my poetry
While loved by some
Does not pass judgmental muster
By literary lights,
As yet another
Writer of bad sonnets
I enter the new year
As I have so many before it
With a bunch of unfinished projects
Declining energies
Unremitting work demands
Economic pressures
And not much to show for
Reams of writing—
Words spread out across the page.

For Anne and Meridel

On November 13, 1915
My mother Anne was born
Now she would be
Eighty-five years old
She died of bone cancer at 47
Tragedy of infinite proportions—
Idealized by all of us
Much of it was deserved:
Extremely compassionate
Wonderful with children
Dedicated to a better world
Intelligent, persuasive, articulate
Loved devising new arts and crafts
From ordinary materials at hand
Frustrated by daily strains
Only able to do a few paintings
No stranger to hardship and stress
Subject to migraine,
Holding too much in,
Radiated quiet empathic warmth
Had a gentle way of understanding
A true connection of the heart—
Then the sudden shock
The awful toll
Meridel spoke
As we sat a sort of shiva
Of the light in my mother's eyes
Her special luminance of spirit.

On the 14th of November, 1996
Meridel ripened into death
As old as the year, at ninety-six
She leaves behind
A body of work
Songs of the spirit
Writings of so many kinds
Children's stories
Global poetry
Voices of Women
Most oppressed, the People
On the prairies of democracy
Solidarity wherever in the world
The Freedom River flows
A long and lucid life
Lessons a woven blanket
Of Native wisdom
And relationship
Shy yet indomitable
She leaves behind
A fierce and loving clan
Commitment to struggle
Compass of guidance
Amidst imperial onslaught
Resolute resistance against
The daily decay of greed
Her own luminance of spirit
Shines like harvest moon!

Sweeping Ode to Lisa's Holiday Brooms

Amidst your stuff make elbow room—
There's always room for one more broom!

They say a new one does sweep clean
Now what exactly does that mean?

It seems to me new brooms must learn
Just how to work and where to turn.
Old brooms don't die, may lose some straw
But know the contours of the floor.
Seek crannies where dust devils hide
Clean corners where the scum reside.
Old brooms may not have bells and whistles
But pass on lessons to new broom's bristles.

That said, we also hail the new
And gift this brand-new broom to you
Paint rainbows, hang charms all about
May broom sweep out all fear and doubt
Brush aside the growing grime
Of tyrants spewing greed and slime
All of their detritus cast
Into the dustpan of the past!

For New Year's may we bend an arm
To keep the gentle safe from harm
Clear off the cobwebs of despair
With clarity of love and care.

So take new broom and use it well
Who knows the stories it will tell

May your best wishes sprout and bloom—
There's always room for one more broom!

Note: One Christmas Lisa, my wife, handicraftily and
beautifully painted some special brooms for family and
friends. This poem accompanied the great (and useful) gift.

For the Millennium

Finishing up
Two thousand years
I cast about
For reassuring signs.

Stormy weather
Rainstorm after rainstorm
My back's in spasm
Too much work!

What a struggle
Sometimes
Just to keep it all
Together—
Know what I mean?

Regardless
Life spirit surges
Ceaseless, unremitting,
Incredible spark
Of self-consciousness
Amidst a Universe
Of infinite expansion
That also is contracting
Or may be composed
Of giant bubbles...

For the millennium then
These humble homilies:

Think about what you want
Not about what you don't want.

If you don't know what to do,
Don't do it—my father said.

As Wilbur Broms advised
"Create works of lasting value."

And Meridel Le Sueur counseled
"All our words have meaning and give light."

311

Gary Snyder pledges:
    "...allegiance to
    the soul of Turtle Island
    and to the beings who thereon dwell
    one ecosystem
    in diversity
    under the sun
   With joyful interpenetration for all."

I'll pledge to that!

For the millennium then
May it come to pass—

Some simple things:

First, that the entire Earth
Every nation, state, city, town, and village upon it
Implement the United Nations accord on
The Universal Rights of the Child.
Let's take it from there...

Millennium demands
We rid the Earth of all weapons and warfare
Which presupposes Justice and Democracy
Which can only be achieved
Through radical redistribution of wealth
Equality of gender, race, ethnicity,
Millennium demands
Emergency efforts to restore
Global environmental sustainability

Millennium, my friends, demands
Realization of the Links of Love
Central to all spiritualities.

Finishing up
Two thousand years
I cast about
For reassuring signs.

And then, on September 11, 2001

an event

of great tragedy and terrible loss of life

an event

with sudden, severe, shocking consequences

that continue to reverberate

triggering a tectonic shift in the

plates of international relations

in the faults of poverty, racism, sexism,

amidst the awful roar of greed and militarism

a major earthquake

tidal wave/tsunami still rolling

threatening to engulf us all…

(It's what they call a turning point…)

September 11, 2001 by E.A. Poet/Lincoln Bergman

The eleventh of September
We are certain to remember
Babel's towers crashed colossal
On Manhattan's teeming shore
People leapt in desperation
Facing instant immolation
Flaming fuel of aviation
Shook a nation to its core.

Upon that mournful morning
Death struck without a warning
Our minds in shock unending
Throbbed with numbing roar of war
Like lightning bolt and thunder
The whole world blown asunder
Nightmare television image
Things we'd never seen before.

So many people slaughtered
Mothers, fathers, sons, and daughters
This one word, "terrorism"
Is on everybody's tongue
Nation reels with losses tragic
Horror hemorrhagic
Heroes face the flames of fury
Patriotic anthems sung.

The eleventh of September
World is certain to remember
When lion of the Pentagon
Lay wounded in his den
Now he roars in rage and panic
His armaments titanic
He will punish evildoers
Bomb to bits the Saracen.

Does Bin Laden bear the blame?
Take a look at whence he came
Fundamentalist fanatics
Funded by the CIA
Like Saddam Hussein before him
He now bites the beast that bore him
On his head they place a ransom
They will make the whole world pay.

Mobilize U.S. attack
Maybe finish up Iraq
(That's been on the agenda
Since dad sat on the throne)
Every week more children die,
Blockade the reason why
Spyplanes circling like vultures
To feast on flesh and bone.

Twist both arms of Pakistan
Take out Afghan Taliban
There, where lines of land mines
Run a flood incarnadine
As Israeli occupation
Exploits the situation
To step up assassination
On the soil of Palestine.

Rapidly the cauldrons boil
In a torment of turmoil
Drums of war are beaten
Flags of pride and fear are flown
As they launch a new Crusade
Paths of reason seem to fade
Oil transmuted into blood
Crimes that no god can atone.

It was on the same sad date
When a free Chilean state
Was so viciously cut short
By Kissinger and crew
To gain justice in our times
All who perpetrate war crimes
Must be brought before the people
To receive their earthly due.

As in Vietnam they said
As they left more millions dead
We had to bomb the country
To save it, can't you see
Will that also be their plan
To save Afghanistan?
The ghosts of Nagasaki
Gaze down in empathy.

The eleventh of September
World is certain to remember
The "century's first war"
Bush rushes to proclaim
Names network of Bin Laden
Never mind the Earth's downtrodden
Vows to smoke out every terrorist
Set the globe aflame.

Civil liberties rear-ended
Rights of speech suspended
Congress rolls right over
One brave woman who dissents
Seal up each and every border
Hail the same-old new world order
Use the anti-Muslim frenzy
To repress all discontents.

Yes sadly we'll remember
The eleventh of September
Long after every ember
Has turned to ash of war
In this tragic bitter hour
Can we somehow find our power
Work for peace with every fiber
With the world say—War No More!

The eleventh of September
We are certain to remember
As with sorrow, pain, and anguish
We pace upon the floor
In the distance hear the chorus
Freedom spirits still implore us
A courageous chant is rising
Let there be war—Nevermore!

Baghdad by the Bay

Years ago, this wide-eyed kid from Sacramento dubbed it Baghdad-by-the-Bay, a storybook city of spires and minarets, gay banners fluttering in the breeze... Herb Caen

Gay banners indeed!
The inimitable columnist Herb Caen
Called San Francisco "Baghdad-by-the-Bay."

Which today gives rise to the thought
That the Baghdad of Iraq
And Baghdad-by-the-Bay
Are filled with living, breathing people
Who have a right not to be bombed
By robber barons, not to be crucified upon a well of oil.

In 1958 U.S. Marines invaded Lebanon
The question my father and some other
Revolutionary artists and trade unionists
Asked then: "Why Die for Standard Oil?"
Was painted on long sheets of paper
Down in our garage—behind the question
A giant drop of oil changed into blood.
Late that night they pasted the banners
On fences all over Baghdad-by-the-Bay
Their clandestine action and the slogan
Made Herb Caen's column the next day!

Blair/Bush

Why is Blair in Bush's pocket?
Do they share a bomb-shaped locket?
Do they share a lust for oil?
Want to be like Davy Crockett?

What does Tony see in George?
Has he forgotten Valley Forge?
Do they share a lust for power?
We should have heeded Eisenhower.

Wolfie Limericks

I attended Cornell with Paul Wolfowitz, Deputy War Secretary,
which may account for my poetic obsession with his ideology.

There once was this wonk Wolfowitz
For Afghanistan gave not two shits
Had his sights on Iraq
To break Saddam's back
And bomb all Baghdad into bits.

Wolf-o-witz, Wolf-o-witz
Wants to bomb Iraq to bits!

A masterful mind we are told
With strategies brilliant and bold
Moving pieces of chess
To take and possess
The world as a U.S. stronghold.

Wolf-o-witz, Wolf-o-witz
Wants to make a Baghdad blitz.

How about a swift kick in the "tush"
Or go jump in the lake with a push
His mind has derailed
(Not because he's inhaled)
He's called "Wolfie" by "good old boy" Bush.

Wolf-o-witz, Wolf-o-war
Philosophy that I abhor!

Wolf-o-war, Wolf-o-worse
Plays dice with our Universe.

What became of that once cheerful Paul
Some youthful cohorts recall
He's turned into a sword
Of dread and discord
Dripping with blood, oil, and gall.

Wolf-o-witz, Wolf-o-witz
Terrorism he commits.

Wolf-o-witz, Wolf-o-witz
Wants the world in U.S. mitts.

I'd pity this man and his ilk
For all of their satin and silk
If it weren't for the fact
That each deal they transact
Robs children of freedom and milk.

Wolf-o-witz, Wolf-o-witz
Call it fascist if it fits.

Wolf-o-witz, Wolf-o-sheep
Arrogance makes my skin creep.

Friends, I'm appealing to you
To help figure out what to do
Our own Bill of Rights
Is in their rifle sights
This is a real right-wing coup.

Wolf-o-Witz, I knew him when
How could I imagine then

What can I say at the last?
When this evil axis has passed
The whole world will smile
In much finer style
Our sense of relief will be vast!

He'd appear on war crimes signs
Spout big lies like loose land mines.

Brilliance, when it lacks a soul
Can dig a road-to-Hades hole.

If Sharon's a Man of Peace

If Sharon's a man of peace
Tigers don't have any teeth
Vultures do not feast on meat
Sweet is bitter, bitter's sweet

If Sharon's a peaceful man
Bombs don't hit Afghanistan
No hatred in the Ku Klux Klan
And Clark Kent isn't Superman.

If Sharon would kill no one
Plants would never seek the Sun
A woman's work be quickly done
And Hitler was a lot of fun.

If Sharon's a man of peace
Dogs love cats and pigs are geese
Birds have fur and mice have fleece
And Black youth need not fear police

If Sharon's a peaceful guy
Guns don't shoot and birds don't fly
FBI don't mean to pry
And Palestinians don't die.

By now, I'm sure, you know the score
Sharon's a bloody man of war
The only way for peace to shine
Is independent Palestine.

Baghdad: Embedded Sonnet

These mosques and minarets of ancient fame
Have seen their share of wicked whips and war
But not before subjected to such shame
Such massive might, barbaric to the core.
Had this been London, Melbourne, or Madrid
Had this been peaceful Baghdad-by-the-Bay
The networks would not cheer-lead as they did
Instead with outrage they'd inform our day
But these are Arabs, call them all Saddam
Sand-skinned Semitics if the truth be known,
So racist taunts are etched upon each bomb
Stain every flap of flesh torn from the bone.
Yet conquest we remember after all
Embeds imperial decline and fall.

Song: O Little Town—2002

News Report, April 3, 2002: Holy places were not immune from violence that raged the length and breadth of the West Bank. Palestinian defenders were inside the Church of the Nativity in Bethlehem, built over the grotto where tradition says Jesus was born. About 20 of those inside the Church were wounded and being tended to by nuns, according to witnesses trapped in the church compound. All have been denied access to ambulances or hospitals.

O tragic town of Deathlehem
How sad your streets run red
The occupier's juggernaut
Is piling up the dead
Yet in your spirit shining
The everlasting light
The hopes and fears of all the years
Are met in thee tonight.

For Christ was born of Mary
Right in this very shrine
Now Church of the Nativity
Holds wounded Palestine
O nations, all together
Proclaim the gospel song
For peace you see can only be
When Justice rings out strong.

How violently, how violently
The tanks and guns take aim
A bitter tide of genocide
Sets all the world aflame
Yet people can build bridges
Solutions can be found
Yes everyone can share the sun
Upon that sacred ground.

Then children, healthy, happy,
Could play and go to school
All faiths and creeds could put in deeds
Compassion's golden rule
Where Tolerance stands watching
And Truth holds wide the door
The hatred slakes, the glory breaks,
And Freedom rolls to shore.

O precious child of Bethlehem
For you we must demand
An end to occupation's lash
In fabled Holy Land
Then choruses of millions
The great glad tidings tell
All eyes will shine as Palestine
Rings out the Freedom Bell!

Note: This song is much modified from the 1868 lyrics by
Phillips Brooks for the Christmas carol. A few lines are the
same. The five verses parallel the verses of the song, even
though most of us only know the first verse that ends "the
hopes and fears of all the years are met in thee tonight." In
many ways, these fears and hopes are "met" in the Middle
East today, in the genocidal war waged by the Israeli mili-
tary, in the ongoing resistance of the Palestinian people to
colonial occupation, as in:

Jenin

Now this town too
Like Guernica and Lidice
Like Deir Yassin
Must be added to
The list of genocidal graveyards
Occupation's hazards
Colonialism's curse—
But this town too
Like the Warsaw Ghetto
And Tal-al-Zaatar
Will be added to the honor roll
Of places where resistance
Rose to unassailable heights
The name Jenin will be proclaimed
On independence day.

If I Could Paint...

If I could paint
Picasso's dove
Or coat the Earth
With tender love

Then on that day
Of lasting peace
The shouts of joy
Would never cease

Then we would fly
To that warm place
Where all the races
Do embrace

Where all the creeds
Plant seeds and dance
Where every baby
Has fair chance

Where women
Need not fear the dark
Where children
Frolic in the park

Where men express
Their gentle side
Where old folks
Walk the world with pride

A world where kindness
Greets the dawn
That treasures poems
Like gentle fawn

A world connected
Like a quilt
With weave of love
Not greed or guilt

Where doves of peace
Fly high and soar
Where justice rolls
On every shore

A world where freedom
Is the song
Where might's not right
And right's not wrong.

That's the world
I want to see
I'd like to think
That you agree!

Closing Prayer   (April 1996)

I turn to the East
Where the Sun rises and the day begins.

I turn to the West
To the Ocean
Source and Mother of all Life.

I turn to the South
To the tropical rain forest
All plants and animals.

I turn to the North
To the North Star of Freedom
For love, family, friends, compassion, justice, peace.

Chants Finale

These are my chants finale
These are my final words
Before I can contain them
The rhymes fly out like birds

Always go together
One leads to another
If one line is a sister
The next one is her brother

So I keep on rhyming
Rhythm has no end
Time a river winding
All around the bend

Space a place surrounding
Earth a cradle nest
Life a gift of glory
From its worst to best

Never-ending story—
There are no final words
Before I can contain them
The rhymes fly out like birds.

End Note: It's time to end this book—as I write this, first in the month of October 1996, and now in May 2003. At some point or another one has to come to a conclusion, even though, as Meridel once told me, there are really no beginnings and endings. In my late teens, I was telling her about a book idea, but just wasn't sure where to start. She laughed lustily and told me to start anywhere, there was no beginning and no end. "Start," she said, "with the ocean crashing on the shore…" Wise words within the time-space warp continuum…on this infinitesimally tiny nook and cranny of matter in a pulsing Universe.

I have been partly responsible for the conception and birth of many educational and creative volumes in my time. The ability to encourage others is a very rewarding calling. I am good at motivating other writers to create and produce good works. Sometimes those works become partly mine. I guess workwise I am particularly enamored of the science theatre plays I've helped write and the GEMS teacher's guide entitled *Investigating Artifacts.* I'm a decent editor, and once upon a time was even considered an excellent proofreader and fiery radio announcer. But that was once upon a rhyme.

If this book serves to remind us that, as Charles Dickens said, "life is given to us on the definite understanding that we defend it to the last," that would be sufficient. If it also brings back some meaningful memories and reflects some tempestuous times, so much the better. We, this country and the entire planet, face very difficult struggles ahead. May we evolve as a species and a worldwide popular force to overcome the beast whose teeth have already stained the century with blood.

I want to thank all of you who have had the kindness to read these poems. They were written for the people I know and the times, and perhaps some have touched a resonant chord. I am truly grateful that you have taken the time to accompany me on this journey through these chants of a lifetime. Dear reader, whoever and wherever you may be, I bid you fond farewell. Or, as the Vietnamese proclaim when saying good-bye to someone close going on a long journey—"the world is round, my friend, we shall meet again."

In Love and Struggle,

Lincoln